The Vicious Red Relic, Love

Sarah,
How do we
as feminists
silence this violent
desire?

a fabulist memoir by
xox Anna Joy Springer

"There is only one Anna Joy Springer..."
– Kathleen Hanna, lead singer of Bikini Kill and Le Tigre

"...Only one. Her words take me from kitten to monster and back again in a way only she can do. I love this book."

– Kathleen Hanna

"How to describe the charm, wit, innocence and energy in Anna Joy Springer's Red Relic? With intelligence and heart she enlarges a little the things of which a novel is capable. How very lucky I am to have read it!"

–Carole Maso, author of AVA and Break Every Rule

"In this compilation of magical eclecticism, Anna Joy Springer converses with friends – some are alive, others dead, and one is made of tinfoil. She unfolds epics old and new, assigns quizzes and instructs us on how to read life and love in a world 'robbed of certainty.' This is a wild ride, a really hilarious, sad and sexy read and I advise you to take it with you wherever you may be going."

– Jack Halberstam, author of Female Masculinity and The Queer Art of Failure

"A page–turner, fast and muscular, electric... The handling of the Sumerian/Babylonian mythological material is superb. And you finally never know, as reader, if you are reading 'myth' or autobiography.

–Alice Notley, author of Grave of Light: New and Selected Poems, The Descent of Alette, and Reason and Other Women

"My god this book is beautiful. Each moment. A breath in a forest, a breathing beneath the bark of trees. A way to see that has remained shadowed, in shadows, under shadows. Each sentence a journey."

– Doug Rice, author of Between Appear and Disappear, Dream Memoirs of a Fabulist, and Blood of Mugwump: A Tiresian Tale of Incest

The Vicious
Red Relic, Love

a fabulist memoir by
Anna Joy Springer

Jaded Ibis Press
sustainable literature by digital means™
an imprint of Jaded Ibis Productions, USA

For Cybele, wise metaforest guide

Anna Joy Springer

Acknowledgments

A long list of friends and mentors deserves a great showering of adoration for their reading, encouragement, and/or endorsement of this book: Aimee Bender, Alexandra Chasin, Ali Liebegott, Alice Notley, Art XX (Aorta) Magazine, Birds of Lace Press, Brian Evenson, Camille Forbes, Cathy Gere, Christine Nguyen, Christine Wertheim, Connie Samaras, Daniela Sea, Dodie Bellamy, Doug Rice, Dylan Burke, Eileen Myles (for EVERYTHING!), Gina Abelkop, Inanna, Jack Halberstam, Janice Lee, Jesse Taylor-York, Juliana Snapper, Karen Garman, Kathleen Hanna, Larissa Heinrich, Leon Baham, Lidia Yuknavitch, LTTR, Lucy Corin, Lynn Breedlove, Maggie Nelson, Manvi Singh, Margaret Hitchcock, Matias Viegener, Melissa Chadburn, Michaela Walsh, Miranda Mellis, Naima Lowe, Nancy Romero, Noah Wardrip-Fruin, Peggy Munson, Rae Armantrout, Renee Gladman, Robin Coste-Lewis, Sarah Shun-Lien Bynum, Sam McWilliams (& for the book-finishing tattoo!), Sidebrow Journal, Silas Howard, Sister Spit, Suspect Thoughts Press, Tisa Bryant, and Vanessa Place. I am also deeply touched by the generosity of the artists who made posters for the color and fine arts editions: Paula Cronan, Kristie Fleming (& for her unbelievable patience and constant love), Shelley Jackson, Leon Mostovoy, Rhani Remedes, Cristy C. Road & Aaron Cometbus, Belden Sezen, Annie Sprinkle & Beth Stephens (Love Art Lab), Teresa Carmody & Maude Place, and Miriam Stahl. I'm extra sappy about Rachel Carns and Tara Jane O'Neil who made the genius soundscape for the forests, in addition to posters. Deepest gratitude goes to writers Judy Grahn, Betty De Shong Meador, Enheduana, Samuel Noah Kramer, Lynn Margulis, and Dorian Sagan whose works on Sumeria, Inanna and life forms were invaluable in my research. Also, much appreciation goes to my most adored, patient, and fierce writing teachers, Kathy Acker, Lyn Hejinian, David Meltzer, Thalia Field, and Carole Maso, as well as Brown University's Literary Arts MFA Program, where this book began. And, of course, thank you so much to Debra Di Blasi and Jaded Ibis Press for bringing this book out and spending so much time with me on design! I am also deeply grateful for the generous support of the UCSD Literature Department and the Hellman Foundation for offering the resources and time needed to write this book. My most enduring thanks goes to the spiritual teachers, Pema Chodron, Thich Nhat Hanh, Eugene Cash, Cybele, and Tara Brach. Finally, I acknowledge my deep love for my mother Marcia Bryson and my father Leslie Springer, and I send out gratitude for their thoroughly weird and brilliant inventiveness and for teaching me that grief is sacred.

Portions of this book have appeared in the following publications:

"The Forest of Clashing Erotics," Sidebrow digital journal, winter 2006. http://www.sidebrow.net/ and, Sidebrow 1 2008 Anthology, at press - October 2008 (24.)

Excerpts in Suspect Thoughts: A Journal of Subversive Writing #18, "Utopia Means Nowhere," Ed. Peggy Munson, winter, 2007.

"Forests," "Goddess," and "Inanna", Encyclopedia F-K, edited by Tisa Bryant, Miranda Mellis, and Kate Schatz, fall 2010. http://www.encyclopediaproject.org/.

"Pneumonic Devices" for ArtXX: Women in Art, Issue 1, edited by Francesca Austin Ochoa, fall 2008.

Contents

Anna Joy Springer

Anna Joy Springer

"Nature is a temple where
living pillars
Let escape sometimes
confused words;
Man traverses it
through forests of symbol
That observe him
with familiar glances."

– Charles Baudelaire

Anna Joy Springer

"All of us were happy
in the forest!
No one there was vicious,
no one porous!"

– Blinky

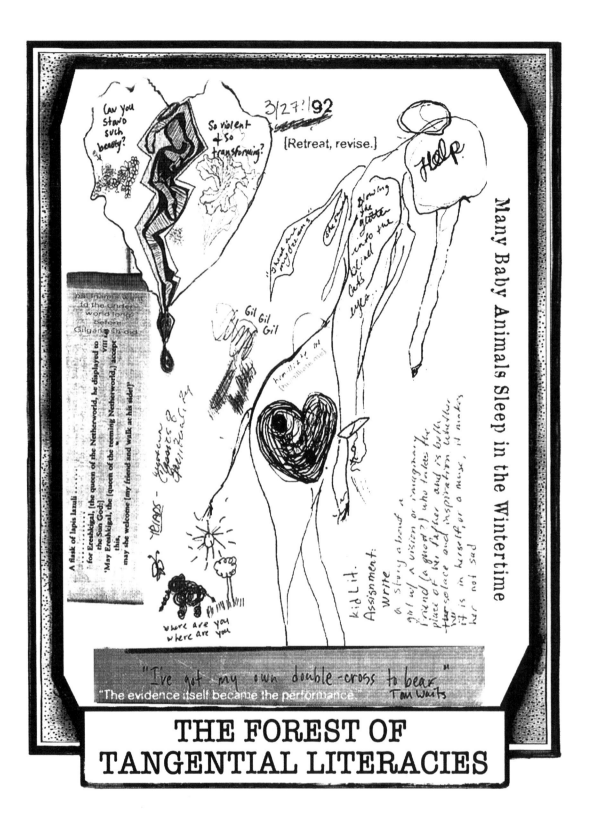

THE FOREST OF
TANGENTIAL LITERACIES

THE FOREST OF TANGENTIAL LITERACIES

Regular history marches forward protected by stories of cause and effect, but not in the Forest of Tangential Literacies.

In the Forest of Tangential Literacies it's possible to go backward and forward in time, even to rearrange time. So that a vein in a leaf may pass through the heart of a poisonous toad, then through a sulking diary, and after that through a thin needle and into an arm, and back to the original leaf before it has uncurled. Desire goes forward and backwards, gathering momentum and discarding it thoughtlessly.

In this Forest it is easy to mistake oneself for one's companion. Or, it feels like being lost in one's own house. Here, one may reach back through years, through the tangled growth, and hand a gift to a former loved one. The gift, possibly a literary device, might help release the loved one from a felt-but-forgotten curse. The loved one may have died long ago, but that doesn't matter. The gift should be a companion, but not oneself or a store-bought pet.

Also, it is important to disguise the gift. It should appear inert, then become transformed by touch, so it won't make its way into the wrong hands. It must get to the former loved one as if by accident. And become her witness without knowing it.

This transference will take place across special wires, transtemporal telephone lines. A historical phone might ring somewhere in the Forest of Tangential Literacies. The phone may look like newsprint or hash oil, but it is a phone.

It is ringing; it wants to be answered.

But in what language to answer the voice from the past? After all, one's memory becomes tangential, too, relative to its prompt. How to read the nuances of tone on the other end, when the face can't be seen? How, even, to find the phone, hidden somewhere in a fungus patch or hovering like a gas?

If it is possible to pass a witness back through time to a friend in peril, it is only possible if one can find the phone and answer it. Answer it in a meaningful way. To be understood. To connect; not be misread. Otherwise the gift falls to the ground like litter, inanimate and useless.

Obviously, attempts must be made, despite the odds.

The sick lover is completely alone. She needs her companion. The stakes are undeniably high.

The phone is ringing. Pick up anything and hold it to your ear, for it may be the phone.

Start with a greeting, then listen.

September 14, 2006

[Gil]

I think I was dreaming of ▓▓▓ this morning. She was stocky again, healthy looking. She was hanging out with her cousin in a bar. They were playing a card game.

I see her like that in dreams, playing cards or pool in a bar with wood-plank walls. Sometimes she's really skinny, but it's better when she's fat. Even when she doesn't care I'm there. Not mad or cruel, just off doing her own thing, saying, "Hey," from across the room like it's nothing.

When I'd awakened the first time, I saw that I'd written in my notebook: "All great love is also abject fascination." [Gil]'s words, not mine. Her psyche had lodged in my dreams and used my hand to write down her words.

Abject fascination, love. Her exquisitely perverse and morbid spin. I get it. The rotten ache made dazzling.

Yesterday I twisted up this little creature out of the tinfoil from my sandwich. It was an absent-minded gesture. I was just sitting here on the couch fiddling, blanking out on the news, but I like the little guy.

I know it's stupid. He's just an externalization or a screen or whatever—but who cares? He seems friendly enough and that counts for something: seeming friendly. Not newscaster "friendly", not "friendly" with inoffensively styled hair. But companionable. Someone to be here with, that's all.

I should name him. What will I name him? He's definitely butch, but like a sort of sweet butch bottom. A little empty. Also kind of flirty, something up his sleeve. He reminds me of something.

Winky?

He seems so sleepy; so am I. All I want to do is sleep and sleep. I almost said, "sleep forever." Hahaha. All I want to do is sleep and sleep forever.

Blinky?

What's the difference between a blink and a wink? I guess a blink you do by accident; a wink you do with volition.

So sleepy.

I can't call him Sleepy. He's cute, but not Disney. Sort of sad. Weepy?

Oh, enough already, Jesus Christ. I sound like a fucking teenager.

It's later now.

I'm awake on Ambien, half-hallucinating with my new figurine on the pillow next to my head, feeling my heart racing icy and thick. Feeling the walls of my throat tighten like some enemy combatant. My body its own militia. Alone and not alone.

So, okay. Here we are. Awake. I will hang out with my stupid tinfoil sculpture and maybe adjust his trunk and try not to imagine things. Pretty horrible things made hybrid without their consent, grotesque and pitiful and gorgeous. I will try. It's a dangerous time for imagining things.

I'll redirect, make my nameless little fake friend a bedtime story. I'll write it in this journal. It'll be a story within a story that just keeps spinning off, like how it's done in *A Thousand And One Nights* to keep the storyteller from getting killed. It'll just keep twisting and turning until it's safe to force resolution.

It'll be operatic, melodramatic, prophetic, proscriptive, manic. It'll be about everything, everything I would leave behind if I were writing a suicide note.

Which I'm not, I don't think.

I'll start now. It'll be – how do the rich people in 1920s novels say it? – it'll be "an amusing diversion."

And if I fall asleep, out of amusement, exhaustion or, more likely, boredom then thank fucking God.

Anna Joy Springer

The Way My Lover Learned To Read

A toddler takes a box of blue-tipped matches from her mother's housecoat pocket. On the box there's a decorative picture of a slender blue woman with wide dazzling eyes, and an elephant wearing a vest and smoking a pipe. A word or two written in white smoke curl above the characters in a frozen celebratory dance. Jenny can't read the logo; she's three.

She pushes the inner box out from its frame as if opening a miniature drawer. Inside are expressionless dolls – thin, blue-faced, inert. She fingers this stack of identical bodies, all of them lying there unnamed. Bright blank faces, blond wood bodies, no arms, no legs. She picks one out and pushes the bed box back into its colorful casing. She knows just how to make the doll spark: Press and drag and lift. The scratch sizzles in air, ignites, a single petal of flame, young tear. She leans back onto her mother whose eyes are closed.

Jenny holds the match like a baby tooth, like some foreign specimen. Her fingernail gets hot. Then, without meaning to, she drops the match.

It falls into the crotch of the book open between her knees. Her mother's eyelids press muscle to muscle, flicker and twitch, and the black head of the match burns a ring into the page. There's a scar on the mouth of a cave – is it a cave, or a hole dug into a wall? She thinks it's a magical cave, and something that says rhymes – a genie, an angel, a bear in a hat – will come out. Nothing moves. The cave is small, but some creature waits there: Potential.

Jenny listens, attentive. She goes inside the cave. She's aware she's not really inside the cave; she's outside, poking her finger into the wound the match burned, nudging the scar's loose edges. She's listening for snoring, for signs of some family inside. A secret

hideout for genteel fox thieves? An endless leprechaun library with green sugar cookies and women in petal dresses who tell stories in squeaky voices? She touches something papery or woody, burnt at the edges. A small treasure chest or a scroll, some ancient instruction? Then, as if by magic, she's able to make out these words:

There is a special crevice carved into the wall, guarded by animal figures. Reach into crevice and find an ornate copper box.

"Name" and "wall" and "crevice". Not "cave" or "fox". Not "burnt".

Then Jenny turns the page:

Inside the mysterious box find a flat blue stone. Carved into the stone is the most miraculous tale of friendship, adventure, and loss.

Jenny's father is somewhere behind her, in another room of the house. He is waiting with his half-tidy 1970s beard. Sleeves folded up, arm hair raised, alert. He's in his quiet house waiting for his wife to die. It should be any time now.

He's straining to hear his daughter's cry. His other children are off at The Church pulling weeds. He waits for her cry. Will she? He wonders if she's even more advanced than the tests have revealed.

Jenny is well-oriented: It's 1966. She's in her house in West Virginia. It's daytime. Her brothers and sister are somewhere else. She's not alone in the house. Her father is back there behind her, and the storybook is in front of her, open where her mother stopped reading, at the page with the animal cave that was not an animal cave but a hiding place for a secret story, in a copper box hidden in a crumbling wall, in a crevice carved to look like the mouth of a cave. Guarded by strange animal figures.

She understands that the story might help her now, but she doesn't know how. The picture in the book shows a rocky crevice with a burnt eye for a mouth, sentinel creatures with bird heads and lion haunches standing at its entrance, the City wall a skeletal gesture.

She sees, beyond the edges of the rectangular pages, a stiff cardboard cover, then her own dimpled knees, then an exotic skirt limply draping her mother's bony lap, then the metal frame of the wheelchair incongruous with its dirty gray wheels, and the air hovering over the floor and its dust and the low wooden ceilings, their slats dripping sap, and out the windows and into the air swarming above the acres of tedious green, into the world beyond nap time and bathing, into heaven, wrapping around the world, before Jenny's birthday, before the trip to the alligator tank, before her baby brother, and tomorrow and her next birthday, too.

Her name then was not [Gil]. It was Jennifer.

September 15, 2006

Jennifer was my first girlfriend. She called herself [Gil]. She's dead now, from killing herself. She had AIDS and was sick with pneumonia, but she died from shooting a speedball.

That was years and years ago, back when I thought everyone should kill themselves as an altruistic act to the world.

I'm different now. I know more about people. For one thing, I believe they exist. For another, I know I'm one of them and we affect each other and are made by our interactions with each other. My attempts to engage, wordwise or otherwise, just sitting there with someone, being with someone at all, I know that's what I am. But, I'm still partly the same selfish asshole I always was. Still needy and lonely and wondering whether it's a good idea to keep staying alive.

About [Gil], I wish one thing only: That she would have had someone, just one friend who could have watched her go. Not someone like me who would have tried to stop her from killing herself. Although I wish that too, but that's a wish for myself, that is something I can wish and wish forever, that's a wish I can keep with me and roll around in my hand like a stone, because I'm alive. So it's not as urgent. What's urgent is the wish that's not for my benefit but for her, the one where she gets not to die unbeheld. Something

or someone who would be with her when she died and would stay behind knowing the truth of her death, keeping the secret alive, ineffable, and in all ways changed by it. And that angel or mighty grandpa or hamster or nursemaid would walk the earth or wherever it lived, transformed by the companionship it offered her as she died.

It takes awhile to go from being a living thing to becoming something else, something made out of thoughts and words that people carry around in their flesh. To turn from a living being into story. It takes a long time to turn into a gift like a delicious pill.

I don't believe in an afterlife and I don't believe in ghosts. But I believe in things unalive being somehow alive, alive enough to be unpredictable and have an effect. I know I've died a couple times and woken up the next day still here.

If whatever dies stays alive in words, in prompts, the way wildflower seeds travel across state lines stuck in sweaters or birdshit, in how another person changes you, in memory, you know what I mean, how people affect each other, change each other, if our effects extend from the earliest stories to the ones at the very end of time, forwards and backwards, if memory is one-dimensional, flattening all living into one moment, the moment the memory makes itself known – in words, in emotion, sensation, a tic, whatever, if that's true, and I'm not saying it is, I'm just making shit up here, but say that's true. Say that's true.

Then in this one-dimensional place, the place of story, the place where making shit up and remembering it comes together, in this place, let's play French and call it the Forest of Signs. In this unruly place I can find my [Gil] and give her the witness that I could not be.

And that's why I'm really writing this story, I just realized. It'll be like a weird sort of divining rod guidebook thing for Winky. So he has something to help orient him when I send him back in time. So that when [Gil] dies she'll hold her beloved friend in her hand. And it will grow warm. And then, with her, slowly cool.

The birds are chirping, but the phone is not ringing.

Life is not a thing
or a fluid any more
than heat is.
What we observe
are some unusual sets
of objects separated
from the rest of the world
by certain peculiar properties
such as growth,
reproduction, and special
ways of handling energy.
These objects we elect to call
"living things."

— Robert Morison, *physicist*

Pick up anything for
it may be the phone.

Anna Joy Springer

How to Read the Ancient or Hackneyed

The Official Version of *The Epic of Gilgamesh* is a regular buddy myth, which means it's about the right way to be a man. It starts out with King Gilgamesh being a fucked-up megalomaniac, systematic and vengeful; he doesn't respect anybody. Why should he? Who could stop him? He's bored and dangerous. Hot.

He takes the pretty braided-hair 12-year-old girls and, just before their wedding night, cracks them open like songbirds' eggs before some regular schmuck gets to them. And he takes everyone's land, he yawns. He doesn't even enjoy it anymore. He's shaking with menacing boredom. The crying and begging. Nothing. These anguished arrows bounce off his robes, and he brushes them away like horseflies.

Everyone hates this powerful sociopath, but no one can do anything to stop him. He's strong, he's rich, he's handsome and merciless. Untouched, untouchable. A loner. More than a man. Too much a man. You get what I mean.

Word gets up to the gods that Gilgamesh has gone berserk. He's half man, half god, but all muscle and might, no heart. He's setting a bad precedent for the ruling class, whose job is to make sure the gods are well-fed.

To weaken him the gods send Gilgamesh a gift. A companion. This may seem like a strange punishment, but the gods have learned that human arrogance can be dismantled by love.

So, the gods send Gilgamesh Enkidu.

Gilgamesh comes to respect elegant Enkidu, because they're equally tough and equally hot. You can tell he also falls in love with Enkidu, sexually or brotherly, who knows, but the intrigue is so compelling that Gilgamesh stops harvesting virgins and even turns down an offer for a tryst from the most famous and beautiful goddess, Ishtar.

Why should he give her the pleasure? He doesn't need to curry favor with her, especially not now that he's got his buddy. He doesn't like that she treats her men like groveling little girls. To prove how much he scorns her, Gilgamesh and his new pal murder her favorite monster.

But before that fateful kill, during their early marauding trips, it's possible that the two adventurers take skinny-dipping breaks between fighting and smelling each other's hands and farting and cracking up. Like I said, this Epic's a regular buddy myth, full of wild battles and intimate firesides.

Jump ahead to a few days after the monster's murder. Long story short, Ishtar gets more pissed than she already was, so she has a hit put on Enkidu. She really wants to get Gilgamesh, but after a lot of familial bullshit and divine red tape, the gods sicken Enkidu instead – which, Ishtar figures, will hurt Gilgamesh more than killing him would

anyway, so she's avenged, and everyone's a winner.

But Enkidu's no idiot. The marauding wasn't his idea. And killing the monster wasn't, either. He tried to get Gilgamesh to turn back, to drop the whole thing. Maybe go back with him to the wilderness where they could take off their clothes and eat bloody meat, grunt. Basically do whatever they wanted to all day long.

So, Enkidu's laying there on his fabulous deathbed, in pain, aware that he's dying because he stupidly befriended a hero. He knows what that makes him. He's learned narrative convention, and recognizes whose story it is. He can't be saved, he's got to die.

He thinks, "I have been reduced to a dramatic teaching device."

In his fever, Enkidu sees the whole arc clearly now, from what will be called his "taming" in the forest to his feverish decline under a fresh linen sheet.

And: "It was a bad idea to trust this guy, with his sweet smelling breath and clean feet.

Enkidu's last word: "Alone."

So Enkidu dies, cursing Gilgamesh.

And Gilgamesh wails, cursing himself.

He loads his friend's body with jewels. He

prays and fasts, night and day. He shames himself publicly, weeping. The pain in his heart increases. He ignores his duties, his warring and stealing. He leaves his job. He makes his way to the gates of the actual underworld, trying to find his friend and bring him back; he tries to undo the damage he's done.

But he doesn't rescue Enkidu from death, and he doesn't die either. This is a story about the right way to be a man, so it hinges on the hero being tamed. By tenderness. This is the quality that, in the end, makes him a true leader, wise rather than brutish. His grief, his regret, a background hum.

March 1, 2006

Dear Winky,

I've brought all these boxes up from the basement to try to find stuff to help you. They're all over the living room, evidence. They're full of my old notebooks, journals, little crap toys, crumpled photos, flyers from shows I played, other priceless/useless ephemera.

It's all stuff you'll need to know from the early 1990s queer punk scene. They're relics of my culture from just before the over-caffeinated Clinton years, in a transitional time of awkward Saran-Wrap cunnilingus, and phones with cords to rip out of the wall. Everyone was a sex worker or a bike messenger. Identity-bars still swirled with delicious cigarette smoke, GA checks were cashed and blown on strippers every first and fifteenth of the month, and white men were dying with AIDS, no matter how good their health insurance.

And I've been looking up all kinds of stuff about Synopology so I'm going to include that information, too.

You'll have to study, Winky. You'll need to be a trustworthy guide, or [Gil] will never keep you.

— Nina

THE EPIC OF GILGAMESH

.... [she] provided for [her] friend.
.... [she] provided for [her] friend,

.... [she] provided for [her] friend.

.........[she] provided for [her] friend.
.........[she] provided for [her] friend.
.........[she] provided for [her] friend.
.........[she] provided for [her] friend.
.........[she] provided for [her] friend.

[she] provided for [her] friend.

[she] provided for
[her] friend.

[she] provided for [her] friend.

.... a wild [friend],
.... for [her] friend.

The Epic of Enkidu

While Gilgamesh lives, he lives with an ache and an urgent drive to cast it out. To turn what happened to Enkidu into common knowledge, mouth to ear, hand to eye. Everyone should know who the true hero is. He knows that the telling can never revive, but it might revise. Might give him something to hold.

Gilgamesh scratches the lines of his muscular tale onto flat slabs of stone and tucks them into special crevices in the wall encircling his City. He calls the poem undying, a gift to his friend, a friend for his friend. The writing's a coded prayer. A spell for forgetting his savagery, his heart. And his big fuck-up.

But, in the early third millennium BCE, writing is a new technology used only for administrative purposes. So Gilgamesh is not yet media savvy.

He can't foresee that in making public *The Epic of Enkidu*, others will read it however they want. They'll change it and use it. They'll create an Official Version. He doesn't know that every act of reading is an act of writing, too.

What he does know, now that it's too late, is clear: He should have offered his own life in place of his friend's. He should have dropped to his knees and pleaded. He shouldn't have been so proud. In that, he failed.

He doesn't inscribe this failure onto the slabs he's piled all around him like walls of a deep well. He doesn't have the words. Instead, he describes the battles, the war wounds.

Everything he writes about love comes out stupid. He cuts that out.

He lists the jewels he lay on his dead friend. He lists obsessively, in verse. He describes how he left his throne to run witless through the wilderness in animal skins, like a beggar. He doesn't write about the ache.

Anna Joy Springer

"When we get out of the glass bottle
of our ego and we escape
like squirrels turning in the cages
of our personality and
get into the forests again,
we shall shiver with cold and fright
but things will happen to us
so we don't know ourselves.

Cool, unlying life will rush in
and passion will make our bodies taut
with power, we shall stamp our feet with
new power and old things
will fall down, we shall laugh
and institutions will curl up
like burnt paper."

– D. H. Lawrence

Can **YOU** Read
The Syn Of The Times?

Synopology's Solution For A Mixed-Up World

Ever Felt Like "Nothing Makes Sense?"

If you are an intelligent, sane observer you have probably come to the conclusion that the instability of life is encompassing and relentless.

It appears that the madness is worse than ever, with all the signs of the world's greatest catastrophe.

You have suspected, and rightly so, that the fields of politics, religion, business, science, media, arts, mental health, medicine, education and philosophy are dominated by deceitful con artists.

These hypocrites offer no solace or solution, but seek only to fight a secret war for the great stores of energetic capital embedded within your individual consciousness. They compete for your birthright as a human being – your free will.

And they are winning.

We are left with no stable guidebook during this period of psychic warfare. Our trusted leaders have been exposed as charlatans, shimmying into line for a piece of the pie – control over your mind.

But you are intelligent and sane, so you don't sit back and let these soul-sucking mental octopi leech your consciousness without a fight.

Like so many of us did in vain, do you shake your fist at the billboards, the propagandist news, and yell, "Enough!"?

Do you promise yourself that not another night will go by while you passively accept your fate as a processing machine for the enemies' nefarious agenda?

Do you try to shut your mind to the myriad swirl of mass propaganda, communications technologies, and the so-called "wisdom of the ages?"

Do you attempt in vain to focus your beleaguered attention on something – anything – that does not vie to own you, to absorb you?

Do you fight like a child against a giant to delay the very death of your conscious free will?

Like you, much of the world is fighting – and losing.

Do these accusations seem extreme? Melodramatic maybe, overly critical, one big pill? Consider the fact that few among us have ever been truly, deeply happy, and that around the world people with different customs and beliefs share a sense of impending doom. Right now.

Be honest with yourself. You picked up this leaflet titled, "Ever Felt Like 'Nothing Makes Sense?'" Would you have been interested enough to keep reading if you weren't searching for some hope? You are, at this moment, questioning the value of your own life.

When you're ready to face The Truth, call us at

Consider these statistics:

1. 47 out of every 100 people over the age of 16 responded to a recent survey, stating they would purchase a personal nuclear weapon if given the opportunity to obtain one legally.

2. Drug use is at an all time high, with dangerous drugs being forced down the throats of younger and younger children so they will "behave" or "test" better in school.

3. Sign-based movements such as feminism, civil rights and anti-imperialist revolutions of every stripe have failed and cannot be revived.

4. 98% of the world's inhabitants are more confused, angry, dissatisfied and hopeless than ever before. They are therefore more dangerous.

5. One out of every two people asked say they "don't know who they are or why they're here." Half again responded, "and I don't care." The 50% purporting to have a firm sense of self and purpose give well-rehearsed answers encoded in their minds by the multi-national conglomeration of sign-control enforcement agencies.

Since World War II, the secretive and unaccountable worldwide industry of semiotics-control has benefitted twelve-thousand percent from these human tragedies. It has become stronger, richer and more unified.

Fact: At this moment, 77% of recognized words also mean their own opposite when used in official public discourse. Take a moment to think about that.

Is it any wonder then that you, a sane intelligent being, find yourself so often succumbing to hysterical numbness in the face of the overwhelming nightmare you are faced with each morning?

Is it so strange that you escape into sexual and consumerist excesses, desperate digital interactions of every sort, intoxicants and medicines, absorbing banal entertainment, self-help, gourmet foods and exotic vacations in search of relief for your despondency, even as the problems in your life increase and your physical, mental and (dare we say) metaphysical well-being declines so drastically that you find yourself entirely absent, as if you are in a state of constant amnesia, thoroughly saturated with the illness induced by the Semiotics-Manufactury for its own benefit?

We who have found true certainty and peace in Synopology know this is not just a temporary phase that will pass.

And you know it, too. That small portion of your mind and will not already absorbed by the forces of sign-control intuitively senses that something must be done to save itself, the species, and the very planet. That is why you have read this far.

Synopology offers a solution. Synopologists understand the root of the world's malady and the way you can rise above the illness and mental pollution of today's society.

Synopology can teach you to control your own mind and will, to transform suppressive signs into positive ones that will bring individuals like you, one at a time, health, wealth, lasting happiness, a firm grip on what truly makes sense, and tools to keep confusion and despair away for good.

1-800-Syn-U-Now for a FREE Uncertainty Test.

Intentional Lacunae

In Gilgamesh's first draft, *The Epic of Enkidu* is just one more way this hero tries to outsmart the ache.

He leaves the most important verses unwritten or chips them away like a vandal. He wordsmiths an ornate crypt for the ache so it will seem lovely instead of infected.

But pressure of heartache forces fissures unpredictably. Stray longings slip through cracks between verses. They come in dreams where language is helpless.

It's the dreams that mess with Gilgamesh, ones where he's holding Enkidu in the forest, and they're chest-to-chest with electricity zigzagging between them.

Gilgamesh wakes up full of love and horror and no one to explain it to.

These dreams revive the brutal throb. They peck at his authorship, corkscrew his redemptive tale. He re-revises, adds another battle, chips away another kiss.

Still the hero tries to win.

March 2, 2006

Winky,

    I'm compiling the Guidebook just as it comes, lies and verifiable facts all mixed up. Because in order to be true, it has to change shapes and intentions like [Gil] did.
    Does that make sense? It has to dissociate. It has to be unknowable, seductive – you know, all fucked up. Not a legend or a sacred script. Not some easy tragedy, predictable and cathartic. Not something to believe in.

               – Nina

How To Leave The Known, Alone

In Gilgamesh's first draft, Enkidu was happy in the forest. He wouldn't have left for anything. Completely self-sufficient, but also a hero.

For the purposes of the story, however, at some point Enkidu had to get from the forest to the City, where he'd impress Gilgamesh with his cunning and bravado, and they'd fuck shit up until Gilgamesh encountered Inanna, and Enkidu died.

Of course, Enkidu didn't realize he was just some emotional trigger in a lesson meant to humanize a tyrant. He thought he was real, meaningful, living his life, pretty content. He didn't realize that his death, that resulted from his extraction from the forest and his civilizing education, was necessary to his function as the hero's tragic prompt.

Neither did Gilgamesh, until he wrote it down. Then everything made sense.

The Beginning, Again

The cave page has a hole in it where the match had smoldered quietly before Jenny crushed it. There it is.

Again.

She knows what ideas the words are making her think, what story they want her to think, and she reads them and reads them, not turning toward her mother who is under and behind her, in her wheelchair, in the den with all the open doors behind.

I'm making this up.

AND:

It's what [Gil] told me.

And Jenny's father is back in the house, in the past, waiting somewhere, not with her but with her, in an epic standoff, the patience electric between them.

Consider The Verb "To Galvanize"

Galvanize: *b. fig. esp. in phrase to galvanize to or bring into life (also to galvanize life into).*

1853 C. BRONTE *Villette* iii, Her approach always galvanized him to new and spasmodic life. **1869 GOULBURN** *Purs. Holiness* xxi. 203. She would fain galvanize the soul into life by sudden shock. **1880** *Daily News* 9 Jan. To galvanise a little more life into the market. **1883** *Harper's Mag.* Mar. A very old inn, that seemed suffering the first pangs of being galvanized back into life and modernity.

Consider the shock of a wholly new world.

Perhaps the Most spectacular change in the history of the universe began around three and a half billion years ago.

Something strange happened to the life-less combination of elements stewing in Earth's waters. Can you guess what it was?

The most remarkable change in the history of the universe was the appearance of life itself. Yet how the scum and moving particles came alive remains a mystery.

Many religions believe a supernatural creator caused life to begin! On the other hand, pagans insist that the universe itself was at one time entirely alive, and may yet be alive today!

Today's best scientists have proven that ordinary *lightning* brought life to the party.

Isn't that shocking?

As an experiment, a handful of objective scientists were able to reproduce the conditions of early Earth in the lab. They electrified a blend of gasses and

"Volition is the name

water with false lightning.

Believe it or not, the jolt of voltage caused special proteins to form. Living things like you and me are made from the same proteins these scientists shocked into being. WOW!

Could it be that all that electricity was set in motion by a supernatural power? Maybe. But no scientist has yet been able to prove that theory. Still, many of them are working on it. After all, paintings of the greatest gods, such as Zeus and Jehovah, do show lightning bolts flying out of their fingers!

Whether life began with a zap from on high, a wayward electrical current, human belief, or even a combination of these things, we may never know. Still, its occurrence truly is a miracle.

How do you think life began?

Write your answer on the lines below in one complete sentence:

_____

_____

_____

_____

_____

Consider The Adjective, "Shocking."

As in human starvation in an era this technologically advanced, or underage girls suicide bombing, hatred of the meritocracy, the slap of unpredictable love, or some mundane upheaval, a hair in the soup.

"The difference between a person and a rock,"

[Gil] argued,

"is volition."

of the game."

Themes of electricity, love,
and literacy begin to intertwine.

How To Imagine The Missing Beginning

Gilgamesh keeps having to rewrite the beginning of *The Epic of Enkidu*. He suspects that the ache is slipping in at the hero's origin, the part Gilgamesh didn't witness.

He tries to find the right language again. He closes his eyes and imagines what Enkidu might have looked like before they met. What comes to mind is his friend's striking differences:

All his body is matted with hair,
he bears long tresses like those of a
woman:
the hair of his head grows thickly as
barley,
he knows not a people, nor even a
country.

No women, no trade, no gods. Running, swift as a gazelle, cunning as a cheetah. He freed the animals caught in hunters' traps, broke the traps, filled hidden pits with mud. He was their protector but also one of them:

Coated in hair like the god of the animals,
with the gazelles he grazes on grasses,
joining the throng with the game at the
water-hole,
his heart delighting with the beasts in
the water.

His hair stretched out behind him when he ran. His hearing, vision and sense of smell was as acute as the four-legged creatures', and his demeanor even more threatening. He was beautiful.

Imagining Enkidu naked and free in the forest, Gilgamesh longs to touch his friend's warm chest. He remembers the curls of hair, the warmth, and he weeps.

It's no good. He chips away the marks he's made until the tablet resembles a rough flat terrain, the origin again destroyed, a damp tactile abstraction.

Gilgamesh runs his palm over it. It takes many drafts, many decades.

Author Fashioning a Companion: Blinky From "The Forest."

down in the streets,
down in the broad streets,
to the orphan

to her companion

which you have given her

after her death through revised inscription,
O holy Inanna sweet is your
praise!

Stylized Representation of 2 Things:
1. Me, making this time machine.
2. Blinky, who's about to enter the story.

This is the Funny Part!

Into the crack cocaine, into the police dogs licking hooker pussy, into the theater of functional free will [memory], a sleeping creature suddenly awoke.

"Hahaha!" said the small red animal, sort of shocked, when he saw where he was.

He had climbed up the stairs at the mouth of his cave, as in every spring. How long had the little guy been sleeping?

His "ha-ha's" trailed off as the elephant-like creature made his way to the corner of Page and Payne. He shook off the warmth of hibernation and began a delighted, shivering dance.

Cold and gloomy San Francisco springtime seemed like a joke, one the animal wanted to share, but where was he, alas!

Which way to turn, up the hill or down?

Keep in Mind

In the little forest all the animals are happy, but not because they are [safe] [literate] [ducks in a row].

No. Wake Up. [Not that.]

Continue. Enter. [Retreat, revise.] Good-night.

They are happy because every day and every one is:

[under surveillance] [fair and square] [amnesiac].

When you wake, you won't remember a thing.

Danny DeVito, The Toy & Small Change

The newcomer wasn't looking for the forest, 'cause that wasn't there anymore. The little unscathed creature was dark red like a really fine cadmium, oily in richness. And he looked like he'd been twisted from foil. He gave the air of a tiny dignitary from a ruined country with a devastated future but so far untouched by it. He watched the fog sweetly puddle toward the sidewalk near his snout. The wrinkly red being curled up his nose that was dangling in piss.

"Hahaha!" he exclaimed. "What is this?"

Then face to face, he met the dying woman who was pinching him between short chubby fingers, checking him out.

"Where'd you come from?" [Gil] asked her new pet toy, not expecting an answer.

"That mannish woman looks like a goodly trickster elf back in my happy childhood forest," thought the miniature who was brittle to touch but turning all soggy with fog.

The goodly elf was no elf at all, she was my first real girlfriend, [Gil]. She looked like Danny DeVito, but I loved her anyhow. How could I not? Her seduction of me in *Nature As A Concept*, when she trapped my leg and then, with her boots pressed hard into my bare calf, and us not looking at each other for the whole lecture about, I don't know, the death of nature in some kind of unnatural human coup.

Then our first date in the scarification parlor, like a dentist's office done up in black, with her gripping the padded leather ladder – the first time I saw her naked back, its dense, packed meat, frying. I smelled it while I watched it blacken, ooze. Thirteen strips like a ladder down the bottom vertebrae.

How could I not love her?

Her stocky rectangular, cottony, ice-eyed exterior. As if the Susan Sarandon of *Thelma and Louise* were sculpted of bruise-colored Play-doh and squashed from the sky with a tap from a giant mallet. But rougher than that, in a hoodie.

She knew how to read ancient Greek and the difference between "etymology" and "ontology."

And she'd run away from home and lived on the streets of New York with skinheads. She'd been a thief and a whore and had experienced all kinds of adventures I'd only fantasized about.

These were the things she told me those first weeks in bed. We lay there in the dark, between classes, talking about all the lies in the world.

I'd never met someone so smart or tough or funny. An expert of Tom Waits lyrics and an accompanying hippity-hoppity one foot to the other Rumplestiltskin dance, she played the magical creature, estranged.

Dying of a secret disease that she didn't tell me about, she acted herself, but which? She hopped from one foot to the other and stayed awake all night listening for intruders, tweaking into the night while I slept, unconscious. And sometimes she danced a naked choreography around the room when the cassette looped back to Waits', "Small Change got rained on with his own thirty-eight."

Yet

Can Tyrants but by Tyrants conquered be and
Freedom find no champion and no child
such as [dead female splayed]
saw arise when she
sprang forth a [butch with sexy lip ring]
armed and ["]undefiled["]?
Or must such minds be nourished in the wild deep in
the unpruned forest 'midst the roar
of [memories not to be trusted],
where nursing Nature smiled
on infant [made up lie]? Has Earth no more
such [foetuses] within her breast?
Or must such minds be [galvinized] in the wild?"

[*Which* wild?]

Anna Joy Springer

How The Wild Gets Tamed By Whores

At some point, without meaning to, Gilgamesh crossed the tricky line between recollection and fabulation. He closed his eyes and saw his friend in the forest again. He imagined each line of light curve around Enkidu's muscles, the stretch of his flesh, alive, the dank scents.

What he couldn't figure out was why Enkidu left his idyllic home and went to the City. Fine rhetoric wouldn't work – Enkidu didn't know language. Riches wouldn't work – he had everything he needed. Appeals to his masculine desire to fight a worthy opponent would fall flat – what could weaken this self-sufficient brute?

As Gilgamesh transformed Enkidu into a fictional character, he became one, too. Split from himself, he wrote:

Gilgamesh, before he ever met Enkidu, had prophetic dreams of the wildman drinking from a watering hole on his hands and knees alongside the four-legged animals, with the tips of his long hair dipping into the water.

All of a sudden he realized what had tamed his friend. He saw what happened there at the side of the watering hole. It had taken a go-between, a conjunction, something close to the earth, but knowing the way to intervene. A tricky persuasive teacher, half-animal, half-man.

So, a common whore taught Enkidu language, and that was his ruin. She oiled his hair, perfumed his thighs. Taught him to write his own name in the dirt.

Stunned when they heard Enkidu speaking, the other animals hid themselves. He had become like the trap-setters.

Then the whore and priestess Shamhat lured Enkidu to the City. It was, after all, her job.

She told him a despotic king was there. All the traps in the forest were set to dress the table of this savage. Often he'd send whole carcasses back to the kitchen, untouched, to be thrown to the dogs.

In conjuring Shamhat's voice, Gilgamesh listed his own crimes. It was the first time he'd thought of his actions that way. But everything she claimed he did was true.

Enkidu was sickened by the story he heard. He left the forest to find Gilgamesh, to find and kill him. Enkidu was, above all, a just man.

Gilgamesh wrote, "The wildman did not expect to meet his heart's true friend. That caught them both off guard." Then he chipped that last line away and set down his stylus for the night.

In what would become the Official Version of *The Epic*, a common whore led the wild man from paradise.

*She did for the man the work of a woman,
his passion caressed and embraced her.
For six days and seven nights Enkidu was
erect as he coupled with Shamhat.*

And then the biggest whore of all – the irrational and jealous Goddess Ishtar – separated Gilgamesh from his paradise of unhindered aggressive power and joined him to unimaginable grief.

But because of the goddess' curse Gilgamesh became an abstraction, a hero. A true patriarch.

This was the point of the Official Version. To make, if not truth, then certainty. In other words, Gilgamesh became tamed, too. Tamed by a whore. Whores enact secret, dangerous truths. By the way, a "whore" can be anything.

And the whore in this case, I'm guessing, is me.

Which One? Pick One:

Are you:

[ ] The Winky [or] The Blinky?   [ ] The Enkidu [or] The whore?

[ ] The Inanna [or] The Gilgamesh?   [ ] Then [or] Now?

Make a choice.

Answer fast.

THE FOREST OF COIN-OP-WELL WISHES

In the forest of Coin-Op-Well Wishes, a wisher whispers to the fish in his strange language, asking about his own death. Tosses a bright new penny over his shoulder and crosses his fingers.

It is lunchtime. The other lunch-hour wishers slump around the Coin-Op-Wells like an earthquake's near, or spies. Old-timer fishies with long curled whiskers wait for dimes, no looking, no telling your wish.

In secret wish chambers the well-dwellers say, "Yes," say, "No," flip over and howl with circular mouths.

Curiosity, in the Forest of Coin-Op-Well Wishes, is mild, like going on a field trip to the sad cement tide pool stocked with old starfish, not a seafaring whaling adventure. It's a set-up, so tame it's dangerous. Who knows when there on the spot a wish will come true?

The fish girls return from their break with their fish-flavored flakes all gobbled, their good and bad habits, their dim mates jobless and jittery back at home, waiting, rubbing their fins together. The fish girls with their fish women's duties, fish women's wishes, old ladies' morals, like after a war but before the rebuilding. Bright-scaled nihilism that looks like mirth, a sort of calm unhinged decay and a dread to hope for fresh water to gulp, to let spill.

And the wishers flip nickels with heavy confidence, their sense of unease, their curled-up love with nowhere to go, the way they wish to be watched while they touch their own bodies. What they sculpt with their hands will be as smudged as peepshow windows.

All that wishing and watching and never a soul being perceived. Except for that one unexpected time.

And then the jolt, the thrill-despair of recognition, shared habitat, round eye to round startled eye.

April 26, 2006

Hi, Winky,

It's strange for me to have this intimate relationship with you. Talking to guys is a new trend for me.

Lately I've had to interact with men for the first time since my peepshow days. I've spent nearly nine years avoiding them, which was easy in San Francisco. I try to remember they're suffering, too.

In one of the cat piss boxes I found *The Epic of Gilgamesh*. I read it for the first time since college.

I also found one of the first essays I wrote at Alternative University for a mandatory class on being an ally. It was one of those classes where, each week, we discussed another form of oppression in its various manifestations, then students from whatever oppressed group got to speak about their experience without being interrupted, and all the "allies" had to listen. I made fun of everyone in the class until the day on sexual abuse.

Before then, I had that hardasspunk-antiPC-stop-whining attitude, which is to say I was still a giant racist, classist and homophobe with internalized misogyny and anti-Semitism, plus a whole lot of other bigotry and self-aggrandizement without knowing it or caring to learn. But it was identity politics time, and that's what we were learning at Alternative University.

And it changed my life pretty much. I mean, it made me think that some people actually cared about other people. Which turned out to be an important thing to learn in school. I would have vomited back then if I knew I would say this now.

I totally hope I'm not fucking you up by thinking I'm doing the right thing in these lessons, while I'm really being like a nearsighted hippie asshole. I need you to trust me.

Your friend (I hope),

Nina

THE FOREST OF RADICAL UNSKILLED INTENTIONS

It's floral. It's earth-toned. Self-conscious in knee socks. Its coffee is thin, sipped with Valiums, Black Beauties. It's heart-attack city and birth control pills. It's women in work boots, and men with long beards, Holly Hobby, dashikis, *Taxi Driver* and *Roots*.

In the Forest of Radical Unskilled Intentions, it's two hours each way on the bus to the scary end of wherever. Look for the Union label, and line up for gas, cause it's the Bicentennial! Flags droop on overpasses, flags become ash on the news.

It's surviving the bombs and the gas and the refugee camp, then slipping in vomit at the government office. It's sitting on a hard orange seat next to the enemy in Beginning ESL where a well-shod teacher gesticulates wildly as she enunciates, grinning like a predator.

In dark rust-colored offices, hirsute women and doughy men guide children through relaxation exercises. Shag carpets, clay pots and macrame owls.

Parents in jeans with college degrees stand up for their rights at the PTA, shouting, "Education should be so crucial, people, but they want to turn our kids into drones! Cogs in a machine! These kids don't even know they were born naked! They want whatever they see on TV!"

Raised in war-traumatized manic suburbia 1950s, the newly married have dropped back in and bred, pure bliss and disposable diapers. Unlike their Republican parents, they've thrown out their cold war hang-ups. It's all integration celebration exploration now. Let the children lead the way. Cause we said so, that's why. Mother will show where the clitoris is, you should know, it's here. Don't hide yourself, you're big and beautiful.

Plus, it's always a good time to hug your uncle and your other uncle and all the uncles, cause everyone's family here. Now help daddy roll his joint. And off to Central Valley Baptist because it'll be safer there than in a mixed school. There's some Lucky Charms in the cupboard for dinner. Do you feel your chakra glowing? Remember to breathe. I said, "Breathe!"

You're gonna be the one to fix this messed up world, kiddo. Don't take that tone with me, young lady. Don't give in. Don't sell out. Don't tell dad. Don't tell grandma. You dig?

Then the inevitable unpredictable jolt: In the Forest of Radical Unskilled Intentions the collective is falling apart. Someone's lazy, and someone's a narc. Fathers have cut off their hair, sold out, and started to swing. Mothers have sworn off acid for good, divorced, found coke, and started to date. Children eat gobs of melty carob raisins in the bathroom where no one can see them. A son gets sent home for wearing the pink tights and Superman cape he chose for his first day of school, and a daughter sleeps on a pile of coats in the cubbyhole room.

In the smoggy Carter seventies, twenty new American universities open their doors, half of them religious or spiritual institutions. Understaffed, volunteers work unpaid long hours for the good of the cause. To get better and better, freer and freer, more and more "there."

Also, twenty new American religious groups open their doors, half of them educational or self-training institutions. Understaffed, volunteers work unpaid long hours for the good of the cause. To get better and better, freer and freer, more and more "there."

Adults commit themselves to getting in touch and/ or getting remarried. Their children sit on industrial carpets, guarded by pissy teens or Big Bird. Boredom creeps in, then the kids get creative. They play Sunset Strip, eat kibble, and sometimes set fires. Or they practice their lessons, whatever they are.

The Course of Nature

It was the first day of class, "Nature As a Concept." Our one required "science" class was taught by a tall thin man from Nigeria who wore a gray suit even though it was October, the hottest month in San Francisco. All the other Alternative University professors wore therapist clothes or T-shirts, except my favorite who wore navy blue every day in solidarity with the inmates at some prison.

In Nature class, we'd been going around the room, introducing ourselves. We were supposed to say our name, our area of study, and our definition of nature. Everyone said, "trees," "animals," "the country," like good little alterna-cogs. Weren't we supposed to think deeper than whatever was pictured on the front of the brochure? God, everyone made me so fucking depressed.

I introduced myself, "Nina, Literature and Social Change." I knew I was about to alienate myself but was too irritated to keep my mouth shut. Shock ran through me as I became visible. I was paying for my education out of my own pocket. I wasn't playing games, I was trying to learn. The whole reason I transferred to Alternative University was to avoid being indoctrinated.

I said, "Forests and fawns, that's obvious nature. But what *isn't* natural, and how can you prove it? It just seems arrogant to say that what human creatures do is so different from other animals and plants. We protect ourselves, and we live or die."

The Professor said patronizingly, "Ahhh, but other creatures don't fall in love, build cities, buy water, design precision instruments with which to slaughter entire populations. Other creatures don't write down their laws and then create an entire profession to misinterpret them for high fees, Miss. Nature is not producer of abstractions and consumer of symbols."

I started to answer. The Professor pointed his long finger at [Gil], dismissing me.

[Gil] said her name and that she was a poet. Then she said, "Nature itself is a symbol, and it's an empty signifier out of context. Maybe you see a tree and think oxygen. Maybe I see a tree and think prison." She said she wasn't big on the back-to-nature thing because her parents had moved her and her brothers and sisters to the woods with a whole bunch of other city-people. But all the kids felt completely trapped, with nothing to do but spy on each other, light fires, and play torture games in the trees.

"I like trees," I interrupted. "It's not that I don't like trees."

Nature
10/3/91

Q #-1

Thoreau romanticized
the wild by placing it
above the non-wild, or the
human, thereby establishing
a goal or a betterness
to achieve. The betterness =
aloneness with the non human
earth. However this betterness
to achieve is the heightening
of human awareness - a
pole of reference to begin
a higher self consciousness,
and she is continually
distinguishing himself
from the Concord people
(educated New Englanders)
                    Alternativism

   So by going to what is DIFFERENT
to find 'your soul', you achieve
a higher status in your own
mind, and I see it as
humans USING what is
inhuman in the same way
as we use it for physical
protection (FOOD, SHELTER, etc.)
for mental shelter, justification
purly human ideas notions +
needs.

Nature As A Concept:
Response to "Innocence"

"I'm not saying trees are the big enemy," [Gil] snapped. "I'm just saying there're other ways to look at the 'Let's run off to the countryside to find ourselves' trope. It's romanticizing and escapist."

"That's what I was saying!"

"But," she went on, "humans are obviously very different from plants. We have empathy. We have volition. We..."

"Maybe a rock has feelings. You don't know."

"Can a rock decide to go to a bar when it needs a drink? Can it move out of the sun when it gets too hot? No, it cannot. If gravity pulls, it rolls down the hill. It can't pick up and walk back up the hill."

"Rocks don't have legs. You don't need legs to feel."

She was so strange looking. Punk? A lesbian? She used a word I didn't know: "volition." Smart. Really smart. Her hair was greasy, flat against her face like a grown-out mohawk, hanging to her jaw. Her leather jacket looked new and cheap.

"Ohhh," she said sarcastically. "I get it." She gave me a little double-nod.

"But really," I pushed, "how do you *know?*"

The professor pointed to the smug-faced girl sitting to the right of [Gil]. "And now that we have heard so much from the English ladies, please introduce yourself, Miss."

"Nothing is more breathtaking than nature," said the girl, "From a redwood tree to a peacock to a little weed reaching toward the sun from its crack in the sidewalk. That's what I think."

[Gil] flicked a folded-up note at my lap. It read, "From a cockroach, to a cancerous testicle to a mother cat eating her kittens as fast as they fall out."

God she was hot.

Within a few weeks we would move from Western European Romantics like Rousseau who liked the idea of self-guided education but thought women were stupid, to woodsy Americans like Emerson and Snyder. The entire textbook was compiled of men who'd found solitude in greenery sublime and couldn't stop writing about it. "Nature," always in tension with human culture. Never complicating the terms. Never seeing that in saying human culture was so completely different from ant culture or inter-special cultures, they were actually reaffirming human exteriority and, usually, superiority. The superiority of being the biggest jerk is still a kind of superiority.

Three weeks into the semester I was already bored with what promised to be another three-hour group performance of predictable questions and devastatingly obvious answers. I took out my watercolor pencils and started to draw the professor in my notebook. His skin was dark, almost navy. He had very refined features. He was nice to draw, but he kept moving around.

I was wearing a rayon 1940s dress torn at the armpits like all of my dresses. It was the color of a stained doily, with red and blue horses galloping past iron gates and street lamps. Beneath the desk, I could see my dirty ankles, my bare legs. God. Would I ever get my tattoo finished? Or would I just leave it half done, like everything else?

I pulled the skirt up to my thigh and crossed my calf over my knee. Wetting a green watercolor pencil with my tongue, I began to color in the vine and leaves on my calf. The professor was reciting Snyder's poetry,

The phone will start ringing soon.

which seemed simple and bland to me. The professor stumbled, losing his place. God, famous poetry was so predictable. I pulled out a magenta pencil to color-in the berry just above my knee on my inner thigh.

The Professor coughed. [Gil] smacked my shoulder, and I looked up.

"Could you kindly refrain from doing that?" he asked. "It's very distracting."

Doing what? I looked at him dumbly.

"Could you put your leg down, Miss English Lady? And please put your shoes back on?"

I set my foot back on the floor and slipped my feet into my china flats, outraged. Maybe you could boss students around like that at some private academy in Nigeria, but not at Alternative College. The whole reason I chose this school was because of its nontraditional approach to education.

The Professor returned to his recitation. [Gil] reached her leg sideways and wrapped her black boot around my bare tattooed calf. She held my leg in place and looked straight ahead.

Could everyone see? I kept myself still. I was more turned on than I'd been in my life.

She held my leg prisoner for the rest of the class. I tried to take notes on the lecture. I never looked at [Gil]. I acted like everything was normal.

After class [Gil] asked if I wanted to hang out sometime. To talk about our presentation on The Pastoral. She knew I did. Already, she knew all she needed to know about me. Way more than I did.

I said, "I don't want to point out the obvious, but since you're not saying it, I'm going to: You had your leg wrapped around my leg, and everyone could see."

She said, "So why don't you take my phone number and call me so we can get together and plan our presentation."

Also, she was getting some "work done" that afternoon at the piercing shop below my apartment on Fillmore. She said maybe I could come by and hold her hand so she wouldn't get scared.

How To Read A Lovestory

In a heroic tale, whenever there are two so much in love so early on, and whenever that love involves upsetting the powers that be, the lovers may end up together forever, but never in life, alive. As if life is filthy, and death is pure.

The big irony of the really gut-wrenching romance narrative is that it's about how love can't mix with being alive. Since readers are living, true love stories are reassuring: The reason love is missing is life.

The Epic follows the love story format but a peculiar version of it. Remember, it is a buddy myth, meant to teach men the right way to be masculine. It's a guidebook on how to assert one's will – but not too much – and the limits of volition.

For instance you can't go to hell and rescue your friend, then go back to living like nothing ever happened.

Anna Joy Springer

April 27, 2006

Dear Winky,

So, as I predicted, Gilgamesh is just another boring man-versus-man story. Or one of those over-simplified high school notions of "theme." Man-versus-himself, man-versus-nature.
Let 'em both win.
As I always used to say, "Kill 'em all and let the Goddess sort 'em out."

But no. That's not me anymore.

Now I'm completely fucked.

That'd be a good name for a dharma book:

NOW I'M COMPLETELY FUCKED:
A Guide To Prying Open
Your Shriveled-Ass Heart

Would you buy that book? Because I totally would.

Your friend and scholar,

Nina

Robbed of certainty, the whole world *shivered* with potential.

April 29, 2006

Winky,

Winky listen. I'm talking about context. You have to put the whole thing in context. You know? It was the early 1990s in San Francisco. This giant cultural shift was happening. I know it now, but I didn't know it then.

I was busy. Running between bands, school, my neon apprenticeship, and the peepshow. Twenty years old, manic and brutalized, panting with sex and curiosity and ego, all workaholic and swirly-eyed like some half-baked Foustina. Busy and high and self-absorbed.

Now I'm busy and sober and self-absorbed.

The notebooks are a disaster. For one, I almost never wrote the date on an entry page. Worse, I didn't write the pages in sequential order. I wrote some upside down, several pages away from the opening lines. Fuck linearity or legibility, I was expressing myself. No one existed but me, no time existed but now. Some of the pages are part homework and To Do lists, part course notes, sketches.

Then there are these little real-time gems of exchange between me and [Gil]. We wrote dirty things to each other, talked shit about the other Alternative College students, who they were fucking and how. Just dumb shit like that.

But there are these few instances where she's responded in my book — these traces in her actual handwriting. I remember her reaching slyly from her desk to mine.

When I find one of these comments I run my finger over the impression left in the page, made by her hand. On the page I'm looking at now, up in the right corner, she wrote, "Yes."

Do you see it, Winky?

— Nina

attempts
to engage

phenomenon
&

picture

movement

friend/
thou/
I/thou

expression
of law

"pure"/
ideal

Tree
remains
separate -
an "It"

hi hi

[Gil's "Yes"]

do you
have
a cigarette
Gil?

" I contemplate a tree

I can accept it as a picture: a rigid pillar in a flood of light, or splashes of green traversed by the gentleness of the blue silver ground.

I can feel it as movement: the flowing veins around the sturdy, striving core, the sucking roots, the breathing of leaves, the infinite commerce with earth and air — and the growing itself in darkness.

I can assign it to a species and observe it as an instance, with an eye to its construction & its way of life.

I can overcome its uniqueness and form so rigorously that I recognize it only as an expression of the law...

I can dissolve it into a number, a pure relation between numbers, and externalize it.

Throughout all this, the tree remains my object and has its place and its time span, its kind and condition.

But, it can also happen, if will + grace are joined, that as I contemplate the tree I am drawn into relation, and the tree ceases to be an It. "

Q - But could a bus bench be a thou? A dollar bill? A Hamburgler figurine? Why a tree? Which living beings count as thou's? And what counts as living?

Knock Knock.
Who's Thou?

THE FOREST OF MYTH AND STINK

In the Forest of Myth and Stink, there's a long line for the toilet. The bathroom is a series of slits in the ground. The potty (slit) area is a site of unmediated expression. It will become a library of material/ natural history, one of several located in the Forest of Myth and Stink.

The line is long. One might hold one's bowel movement for hours, waiting for the go-ahead to scato-biographically amend the collection. All too often, the area may be sealed before an anxious visitor gets the chance to contribute. Long waits sometimes end in embarrassment. Therefore, hiring a wait-laborer to hold one's place in line is popular practice among the well-off. It is not acceptable to ask the worker to bribe his way to the head of the line. Still, an economy of illicit gifting has become rampant.

Those whose patience and luck have paid off get the opportunity to make history. Pushing unassailable verity from their innermost selves, they excrete their uniquely crafted organic texts, rich in unmarred confession. Some teary young parents hold newborns over the slits and shake them until the infants release liquidy stools. Other guests don't stop at humble pee and poo. On the advice of their therapists, bulimics have begun vomiting into the openings, triumphant. Other guests fling themselves wildly in order to release an even greater variety of natural secretions, while still others flick ripe navel bacteria, dandruff, or vinegary spores from between their toes into the steamy, precious collection. Tears of gratitude slide down cheeks, drip between thighs, and find final rest in the ground.

There's the ten-minute warning whistle, after which the area is cleared of guests. Next, muscular young technicians run in with buckets of fresh earth to pour over the raw data. Finally, the stew is left to ripen or "cook" for an unspecified length of time.

Only after the materials have been stewed, reviewed, edited, and catalogued, will the site be opened to the public for purposes of research and amusement.

Maps to approved library sites are provided only after forest officials have tested them for contagions. Contaminated areas are sealed off, destroyed and "reforested." Forest officials worry that ill-intentioned characters might attempt to break into a site under editorial review in order to add to or otherwise amend the raw data. Some may have even more terrorizing ends in mind.

To lower the risk of such an invasion, "cooking" areas have been disguised as regular wilderness grounds, for instance, "meadows or thickets," impossible to locate without the help of a beast's keen sense of smell. Luckily, animals are naturally repelled by the sites.

In the Forest of Myth and Stink serene meadows cover former shitholes. Who would suspect a pair of young thrill-seekers, untoned and unattractively dressed, of conspiring to use only the miniature pencils and yogurt spoons permitted in the forest, to dig blindly into the earth, searching for off-limits or contaminated data?

Why would such girls waste their youthful hours employed in such thankless – and illegal – pursuits? What could they possibly expect to gain in unearthing off-limit excretions – embryos curled up like fiddle-heads, alien cells, two kinds of cum blended together, and a handful of goldfish bones?

Regardless of their intentions, how unlikely that they would discover the precise location of this unintelligible hodgepodge under the very site upon which they chose to picnic?

How even more unlikely that they would find enough material unburned to attempt to translate even a few meaningful shreds?

Forest officials consider this scenario low-risk, given the unsavory nature of the task.

How To Spot An Official Version

Yes, a whore can be anything, but not every time.

In the Official Version of *The Epic of Gilgamesh* "whore" means "protected official of the religious ruling class." It means corrupt, powerful, sexy. It means feminine.

In 1200 BCE (and long before) whores were clergy. If you wanted to feel connected to the Divine, you made an appointment with a priestess and paid a donation. You left the temple feeling ecstatic and soothed. To enter heaven was literally to enter a priestess. A regular woman could go to the temple but also connect with the Goddess whenever she wanted. That was the belief. The vagina was super-divine. It was called "the boat of heaven" and, as a vehicle, it was the spiritual counterpart to the sail.

All over Babylon leaders in the military branch of government were revolting against the tyranny of the Temple, which was taking too big of a cut of the economic spoils and had too much rhetorical power. The Temple was run by priestesses who were storytellers. They were also, mostly, women. And these women and transgendered people gave sex as part of their spiritual offerings. You can see why the people may have been more inclined to support the temple than the militia. So there were lots of power skirmishes between the two branches of government. You might not think this political revolt could possibly have anything to do with what counted as good literature. But it did, and here's how:

The secular/military branch of government held a contest to combine all the different Gilgamesh poems and produce the Official Version of *The Epic of Gilgamesh*. The Official Version would become the template that student scribes would use to practice cuneiform. The same exact wording and design would be pressed into clay year after year. The winner of the contest would gain authorship status, and people everywhere would know his name. In this way he would become immortal, as all men had a right to be.

The winner was Sin-leqe-unninni, a former soldier who'd become a well-known scholar. He pieced together older versions of the written tale and what he'd heard in various interpretive productions throughout his life. *The Epic of Gilgamesh* was a story of man's fear of death, that was clear, but it also dramatized the age-old corruption of religion.

Sin-leqe-unninni had always thought the most emotionally poignant story in the Gilgamesh cycle came at the end, after Gilgamesh realized he would never be able to rescue his friend from the underworld. Having failed, Gilgamesh became tormented by thoughts of his own death. He devoted himself to searching for an herb that would make him immortal.

Sin-leqe-unninni studied competing renditions of the outcome. In some, Gilgamesh never found the herb. In another, he decided he didn't want it. In the one Sin-leqe-unninni chose, a snake stole it from him. The snake was a reference to an ancient and despised fertility cult that the Priestesses cited as the historical basis of their power.

The judges loved his *Epic*. He had truly captured the deepest meaning of the tale. The battles and conquests were more exciting than ever. The scribes transcribed the Official Version, careful to copy every word just right.

Sin-leqe-unnini's name became famous in Babylonia. Everyone knew his name. In fact, his name replaced him.

Actress & Dancer (…with [her] own .38)

I mean, I didn't even flinch when, after a couple weeks [Gil] told me she had "Multiple Personality Disorder." I thought she was being melodramatic, because she was. We all were. If all life were a stage, let [Gil]'s body be a popular prop.

"Insanity is the only sane response," I said, like a fucking crazy person. I admired myself for not freaking out about anything.

How could I have known how bad these personalities – I don't know what else to call them – how bad they possessed her and drove her from behind the thick curtain of her stature. She seemed so together. You couldn't see it happen but it would, and there a new personality would be while the others waited in the wings, each of them vying for a shot to recreate glittering past roles.

Child-stars leaping from the page like fleas.

They drove her and rode her, throwing her over the bumpy endless terrain of their mismatched currents of desire. Heavy, solid [Gil] was more than a hollow prison; her heart was the seat of arguing souls.

Funny little dancer full of souls. One of them knew she was sick, but no one was talking.

Still, she was fading faster than the rest of us, and the woodland creature who'd only recently come from the forest smelled death on the elf, my girlfriend. I didn't smell it, nobody did, none who would talk, anyway. Except for the crumpled long-nosed red object. The comrade. The animal that came from a joyous forest. He was not carved of wood. He was not built of sticks. He was not a fragment from an ancient Sumerian pot. He was a conductor made of something like aluminum foil.

Back in the forest, the wind and the birds and the beastly songs all sounded so pretty that the animals spontaneously jitterbugged. Everything was instinctual in the pretty forest, including the jitterbug.

There are some of us who believe there's no longer any way to become instinctual. We say, "I'm so sleepy all the time. I can never wake up," but that's as close as we come.

When my girlfriend found the immigrant standing at the corner of Page and Payne, she right away decided to keep him.

"From now on your name is Blinky, and I am your only friend and guide here in the City," she said in softly cracked breath.

"You don't look so civilized!" the fresh sidekick taunted.

Then they fought like dogs there on the street corner until they were very tired and in a heap, and [Gil] got her grin. She liked the runaway. She was a runaway, too. She carried him home without asking.

The shrinking toy was surprised by the hint of annoyance that filled his heart with ironic warmth and connection. In the forest, all the animals are just happy, spontaneous, frolicking. But this place was foreign, angular, new. The creature began to be civilized, then. [Me, too.]

In the forest, Blinky would awaken after winter and climb the earthen staircase situated at the mouth of his burrow, The wild & crazy butterflies would welcome him. But this time he had woken up late, with no gentle alarm.

"The butterflies are tardy this year," thought the snoozy creature, uncurling his long crinkly trunk. "Undoubtedly they are tying their rainbow shoestrings into bows."

But the butterflies were far away, back in the forest. The cave itself was in the speckle-lit forest. There was no sun here, no smile on the sun, no wake-up crew flitting into his cave in funny shoes on the corner of Page and Payne.

"Why am I here?" he asked a passing rat.

The rat snarled, "You ought to know, unless you're some kind of dumbfuck, and dumbfucks don't get anywhere in the City."

[Gil] kicked the brash vermin sideways into a pole, then Blinky and [Gil] high-fived.

The rats in the forest were not thieves, although they performed a scandalous dance from time to time 'cause it made them merry. Everyone loved the ritual.

In the forest there was no evil ruler.

Anna Joy Springer

Syno-Hat: Permanent Damage Or A Shocking Cure For Uncertainty?
By Kitty Calloway

Synopology makes headlines in legal news again today, stating that its patented electrical self-improvement hat does not cause permanent neurological or psychological damage, by sparking mental "sign overlap and displacement." The Church argues that the hat, used correctly, actually improves brain function by jump-starting the brain's naturally occurring electrical currents.

Synopology, a peculiarly American religion founded in 1951 by Madison Avenue semiotics and marketing guru Enron Scabbard, requires that adherents use a simple device called "The Electro-Psycho Sign Defibber and Syn-O-Meter," commonly referred to as the EPSD Syn-O-Meter, or more recently, just the S'meter, which takes advantage of ancient electromagnetic technology to clear its user of mental and emotional discomfort. The device enables a user to track his or her brain's pattern-recognition and formation strategies, and then to retrain the mind toward more efficient semiotic management, and therefore to a more productive, less semiotically encumbered "self."

The S'meter, which according to the Church's critics, looks like an old-fashioned "beer can hat," is worn on the head, with metal cans positioned over the ears. Wires extend from the cans to a clip on the tongue which sends signals to and from a patented brainwave register, which rapidly directs results to a small screen suspended in front of the wearer's eyes. It is reported that the machine not only registers, but retrains neural functioning and sign recognition.

Recent studies conducted by neutral labs have concluded that the electro-magnetic leakage reported by disgruntled former Synopology Plaintiffs does, in all cases, alter the functioning of brainwaves, especially in children under 12.

Hotly contested is the legal issue of whether such altering of neuro-functionality is "harmful."

In fact, a recent memo to the press from Synopology's attorneys states that the slight electro-magnetic leakage into the user's skull indeed may provide the user with secondary health benefits, such as intelligence-boosting.

The 4/14 memo opens:

Small electric shocks, at specific intervals, can relieve a variety of unsatisfactory conditions. Electrical current has long been used medicinally to relax spasmodic shoulder muscles or still a seizing frontal lobe. Electricity is known also to spark movement in the dead and even to animate the inert. Synopology extends the value of this stimulating technology to what has been called "the Spirit". Culling the results of a variety of tests over the thirty years Synopology has been practicing its innovative, quantitative approach to spiritual improvement, we have determined that 100% of those adults and children using the S'meter (of their own free will) score higher on intelligence tests and report increased confidence and certitude in all ares of life..."

The memo goes on to conclude that the Plaintiffs would have been much worse off, had they not practiced Synopology's system of self-improvement, and that the fact that these Plaintiffs now feel confident enough to speak out against Synopology is proof that the Synopology Spiritual Program works.

Had they continued their use of the S'meter, the memo further argues, they would have gained substantially more satisfying results.

The problem is not that the S-Meter "leaked," but that Plaintiffs stopped treatment prematurely.

Counsel urges Plaintiffs to drop the pending suit and return to treatment at a convenient Synopology Lab, as early interruption in treatment may cause serious problems, even death.

April 29, 2006

Dear Winky,

It was a time to challenge ownership of truths. To question *whose rules* and for *whose benefit*?

It was a time to fix the classics and fairy tales so the girl didn't end up saved or dead.

It was a time to be cruel, just to be unladylike. It was a time to take out your tampon and bleed on your skirt. To let your tits hang out at the show. To punch drunk men in the pit.

It was a dirty, hairy, boozy time with a bloody futon in every flat and a clove of garlic up every sick twat. A witchy time and a twitchy time. It was a time of investigating ethics and of lying to each other.

It was a time of twelve-step groups and sliding-scale therapy.

It was time to rewrite the rules. Not like now. Are you getting me? It was magic.

                                              – Nina

Beyond Mere Tragedy: The Urn of The Real

In the beautiful forest where all the mixed-up animals frolicked and the tricky elves entertained them with silly dances and fake suicides, there was a pile of garbage bags filled with flowering corpses of young human girls.

No, no. That's crazy. [That's cheap.]

[Continue] [Verify] [Scrap-heap]

My girlfriend's youth was spent in industry, stuffing the bags. This is what she told me. Stuffing the garbage bags full of the dead girls. Her father, an investor, was jealous and charismatic. Along with Enron Scabbard he wagered on an optimistic new business enterprise called Synopology. While Enron Scabbard disappeared into international waters to run the operation from a small ship, his cronies camouflaged themselves in nature. They built planned communities of log cabins and burnt-out motels. My girlfriend learned all about simplicity and communalism there in the forest. That is what she told me.

To be honest, Synopology is a psychological operation for child geniuses. If you become extremely honest with yourself, as a child genius must, you become "Free". When you're Free, you're in the clear. You can communicate with your Zzzatans, then, and can even command them.

Zzzatans are other people's souls from thousands of years ago. They use our bodies for everything, and they've been misinformed by tricky media, which is why we're all so confused and why we've got to reprogram them. But if you tell even one lie you become ugly or sick, and you have to clean toilets.

Sometimes you type in an office and sometimes you get rid of the evidence – the dead bodies of raped girls or other stupid victims – but if you tell a thousand lies, your father, if he's a minister, writes your name on the chalkboard in the church lobby under the heading, "NONHUMAN".

So, there may have been some murder going on back up there in the hills. And Jenny was always "NONHUMAN".

[Gil]'s father killed her mother when [Gil] was three, while [Gil] was sitting in her mother's lap. Her brother died mysteriously after he ran away from the cult. And there were many, many suicides and so-called suicides. Of course, all this melodrama and crime could never have really happened. [Gil] was crazy, remember. And so paranoid. She thought they'd been following her after she ran away, spying and calling her on the pay phone, threatening her. Throwing her in the back of a white van and gang-raping her as a warning, then climbing up on the roof and listening to her phone calls.

It is possible, I guess, that they fed her a cue to kill herself, way back; or maybe her father snuck it into her instant oatmeal: "This message will deconstruct in 31 years."

How To Read The Ancient or Lost

Inanna is the Goddess of Love and War. She's Ishtar, Aphrodite, Venus. Fucks for lust. Pretty sneakthief. War lover, ringside, mouth full of garnets, spitting. She is Desire and Desire's desire to swell.

If there were an Official Version of the Inanna epic it would be called *Inanna's Lament*. It would emphasize the loss of a woman's great love and the logic of seasons. But Inanna's story is not about seasons. It chronicles a brilliant young star's rise to fame and her inevitable fall. It reveals a privileged girl's battle with depression and addiction. It dramatizes her stop-at-nothing ambition, her rocky relationship and erratic temper. The story peaks as the thrill-seeking goddess nearly fulfills her death wish. It is a psychological thriller.

Early on in the tale Inanna's all passion and will. Never bored of getting her way, she always, always does. She is Desire and Desire's desire to burst.

Everyone loves this fierce force of nature. They make her temples that look like mountains. They bring her their silkiest flax and fattest meat. Kings lay on their faces when she passes. Dogs howl at the sky for her. She scares them, and they like it.

Shrewd and beautiful, she's stronger and smarter than any of the other gods. She knows every mystery and holds the key to every art. She owns every sacred wisdom.

She stole them from her grandfather after getting him drunk. All's fair in love and war.

Whatever she wanted she got, except once. She'd wanted a farmer, but her father had said she would marry the King of the city she protected. Fuck politics. She wanted a pretty farmer, pushing his fingers into the soil, stroking and feeding each tiny seed. The passionate farmer, his hands cupped with water. His orderly oxen, crafty canals, dust in his beard and pollen. A young, sweet attendant with rich soil under his nails.

She was promised to the Shepherd King, not the farmer. She fought her father hard, saying, "Never! Not the shepherd with his course wool shirts. Smell of sheep and goats in his hair." Not Dumuzi, the stranger from elsewhere, the first Shepherd King of her city, Uruk.

If there were an Official Version this epic might be called *Inanna's Mistake*. It would emphasize her lack of trust in her father and how wrong she'd been. It would describe Dumuzi and Inanna's loving in detail but not pornographically. It would melt her defiance in the warm grip of love.

But Inanna is Desire, and Desire's desire for disguise. So this is an epic about a change in the political landscape of the day, where military power was taken from the local farmers by sheep-herding nomads from far away. It is a veiled fable

of political intrigue.

Dumuzi went to her, offering black wool, white wool, honey cheese and sweet milk.

She raised a fist to hit him. He stood where he was.

He said, "I am more than good enough for you."

She lowered her hand, paused, and then, like lightning, she punched Dumuzi in the mouth. She didn't run off and get him a wet rag. They stood there eyeing each other.

On their wedding night, their sex was so gorgeous, so transcendent that Inanna created a new law. The courtship would be reenacted every year at planting time. The City would throw a big liquored-up meat-eating shindig with a parade that ended at the Temple, where the King and High Priestess would perform a dramatic recitation of their courtship poem, describing the famous seduction. Then the King would make a big comical show of preparing himself for a long night of pleasuring the Priestess. And after the two political leaders entered the Temple and shut the heavy gates, all the regular people would go home and play Inanna & Dumuzi. Drunk, through unpaned windows, they would howl and laugh.

The yearly ritual would ensure a good harvest. It rewarded the workers and displayed the wealth of the city. It was the

most important ritual of the year.

That's how good it was, those first days in bed with Dumuzi. Now Inanna understood what it was to be doubly alive, a two-hearted being.

But Desire's desire to replicate exponentially pried Inanna from her bed. Whatever she wanted she got. And she wanted to know what it was to be dead.

So she took herself to the underworld and died. In dying, she lost all her superpowers and her beauty, all her knowledge, every weapon, every defense. She was stripped of dignity. Covered in puke, she begged to be allowed to stop dying. It was the first time she had ever begged.

She did not die skinny and swooning in bed. She died in a lump of begging, suffering meat. Her skin was hung on a hook on the wall like a hunting trophy.

But since she is a cunning heroine, she tricked her way out of death and returned to the world more resplendent and powerful than ever. And then she left again.

If there were an Official Version this epic might be called, *Inanna's Rebirth*. And because official versions take the most dramatic elements of a restless tale and slyly invert them, *Inanna's Rebirth* would emphasize her sweeter, more submissive nature as a result of her new understanding. It would emphasize her renewed fertility and motherly cheer.

Of course, there is no Official Version. There is no *Epic of Inanna*.

In truth, when Inanna came back to life she was chilled with a sense of unbridgeable separation. Impossible sorrow. She had no way of speaking to anyone, nobody said the right thing, nobody knew. She was scared, like she'd been at the final gates.

She went to find Dumuzi. And there he was, perched under the apple tree, flirting with girls as if it were any other day. He was not grieving her death. In his lightness, Inanna watched her absence thicken into a form that he misshaped. And Desire desired so fiercely to remain intact.

Inanna had Dumuzi killed. She sent him to take her place.

And that's when she learned the truth about death.

The Official Version would emphasize Dumuzi's attempt to escape from the Death collectors. In verse and chorus it would describe how Dumuzi's sister loved him so much that she offered to substitute herself for him half the year.

The Official Version, fossilized for tame curriculum and government-sponsored festivals, would play up this sacrifice, making it saintly. The sister would live above ground in fall and winter and relieve Dumuzi in spring.

The Official Version would demote the Goddess of Love and War back to a revered but boring fertility Goddess whose amorous happiness upon her lover's return would make flowers red.

The Official Version would never mention Inanna's disappearance. That truth would remain intact, untold.

Erotic Poetries   Class #1
                              2/1/92

FROM INANNA - The Courtship of Inanna &
                                  Dumuzi

- apple tree & wonderous vulva
- Brother Sun God Utu makes
  wedding sheet

Dumuzi (shepherd) vs. FARMER
   CREAM   vs.   GRAIN

of herd / dependency is unattractive to I.

product of ♀ opposition = desire

- Symbol of vulva / boat — Narrenschiff
    boats being vessel which
    carries one accross the
    plural + omnidirectional path - H_2O

- Seduced "Before (her) Lord
Dimuzi " by "plants"

Shining - light - sparkle - glitz —
   ALWAYS ATTRACTIVE

Inanna calls for marriage bed

symbol
of
Inanna →   gate
                post
                at
                door
                ways.

**Notes on Erotic Poetries
Class on Inanna and Dumuzi**

February 4, 1992

I'm so furious. I just learned in Erotic Poetries that the first ever poet claiming authorship was A WOMAN.

That's right. A woman. And not an anonymous one.

Other people wrote poetry and stories before that, of course, but she was the first one to actually sign her name to her words and call them hers. And nobody knows that. Her name was Enheduanna, and she wrote poems about a goddess named Inanna.

Inanna was another name for the Goddess Ishtar, who later became Aphrodite, then Venus. Inanna was the morning and evening star, Goddess of Love and War. A sign of terrible, unstoppable passions. And Enheduanna, the priestess poet, loved her. She wrote to her, even though she was officially supposed to be writing about some other god, some guy, the mascot of the city where she was a big-deal priestess.

Why doesn't anyone know the first poet was a woman? Why am I twenty-one years old and I don't know this? Our whole history. Oh yeah. I forgot. It's all been systematically, institutionally erased from memory, as if it never existed.

Women wrote? People actually read their work and knew their names? Where's the evidence? How many female poets can you name from before the 19th century? So they must not have existed! Presto! With logic like that you could run a small world.

Yes, I do believe it's a conspiracy. An unconscious conspiracy is possibly even worse. And I AM going to call myself a man-hater. As a political act, I'm calling myself that. First because they're hateful and there's something mentally or genetically wrong with them; and second, because even though not all of them are rapists and misogynists it's still considered the worst thing in the world to be a man-hater. For sure WAY worse than being a misogynist, which is basically so normal it's invisible and you seem CRAZY when you bring it up.

And even though I'm just using a word, not screwing up everybody's lives with war and institutionalized oppression, it's still the most venomous thing you can call a woman. It makes all the other women – her supposed "sisters" and "allies" – flee from her side, afraid they'll get called man-haters, too.

Because a man-hater gets zapped. There's nowhere for her to go to register her complaint because men and their dependents-slash-protectors will kick her out of the city walls and she'll have to beg by the gate. Only she won't beg, because she won't have learned her lesson and become submissive. So she'll go out in search of a place to be free from the penis-waggers and the penis protectors, and she'll find herself an ugly cave in the desert, eating lizards and not having any friends. That's what they want you to think will happen to you if you're a man-hater.

They tell stories about what happens to bad girls even as they erase all the amazing history of women and girls.

Another thing I just learned they've covered up is that whores used to be sacred. In the temples! They were like the nuns of ancient times, and there was nothing wrong with fucking; it was NATURAL and even HOLY. People went to the sacred whore priestesses so they could get close to divine Goddess who worked through these women.

Back then people did not see women as crazy melodramatic sluts and build a whole civilization to scare us into shutting the fuck up. Enheduanna, as High Priestess who was also the first author in the WORLD, most certainly oversaw the temple whores.

Back then in ancient Sumerian times, people used to think women were important. Monotheism undid all that.

The Patriarchy lovvves Monotheism.

The Villain is coming,
but he's a distraction.

"Life is something edible,
lovable, or lethal."

– James E. Lovelock

THE FOREST OF CLASHING EROTICS

THE FOREST OF CLASHING EROTICS

In the Forest of Clashing Erotics, you can't tell who's winning, but you know it's a war. It's elemental. On one side it's cloudy, dark, and dripping. On the other side it's brassy, crackling, hot. Place your bets, grab a beer, the curtain's lifting. The show's a tacky woodsy melodrama, like gas station incense. Hear the dripping, the dank yippy plopping, steady dull erosion. And the cliché tango of the crackling flame also snapping, spreading, softening, until the two – the dampness and the heat – are forced to exchange forms, and the droplets become gaseous, the flames liquid. It's divertingly unrealistic, sugary and catastrophic. It's impossible to turn away.

Bambi jerks to a stop, sniffs the air. Flame shoots up a pine like panic. The sap pops, sugar burning and a smell of gin. There's the wild piano rollick of the snapping, dripping and hiss of newborn steam, gay party music from some cartoon time, hysterical out-of-tune notes crashing down. History makes markings on the trees, burns yeses and noes, and I'm not sure, and it's too late in a series of signs in the bark, round black burns in patterns that look like mistakes. Over-inscribed trees crash down, black ribs.

The fucking war, the mating dance, you call it nature, I call it theater. Feel the lure of the overwrought lie: Pretend it's your own secretions on fire. Go into the cave that's the mouth of unbeing and find your worse self there and lick it, extend a carrot on your palm, a sugar cube. Feel your tongued, unlovable self grow rubbery green then burst into steam. It's that kind of forest.

The fire's multiplying like a gluttonous virus bingeing on cells. Hot moisture is breaking apart, floating, gathering forces. Fern leaves are curling, green snakes are bowing, red deer are racing, young girls are screaming, fat bears are melting, a sad savior pops.

Each battle comes and ends so fast, oh no, oh yes, and this is not the climax, no, this is just the beginning.

The steam forms clouds that gather into character shapes. A father is born, fully grown, all stout and played out. Somebody's God is watching, too, slothful, perverse, small hand on round gut. A cloud mother deserts her cloud infant who is dressed as a clown with a clown's drunken nose. She gets in her car and drives deeper into the Forest, bursting, cause and effect, in a shower of shame.

Also, famous cloud-characters from outside the family make surprise guest appearances. In the air above the raging forest fire there's Karl Marx looking harried, selling Jenny's jewels, and there's Indira Ghandi, Winnie Mandela, Jackie Kennedy, and Melinda Gates. All of them running away from the fire, this way and that, slamming into each other like the three stooges. There's Andrea Dworkin swapping sap with Larry Flint. Yes, there's regular porn, well-timed castration. There's dripping, there's devils, there's shopping, there's twelve years of gestalt therapy and a Happy Birthday party with a missing birthday girl, everyone running around like doomed ants, waving their opinions around, taking out their tits, wagging their tails and cheating toward the camera. There's precise technique and dirty cops and psychopharmaceutical reps. Plus that dripping, that enemy licking, that mushroomy funk.

In the Forest of Clashing Erotics what makes you sick also makes you're body stiffen like a unicorn's magical prick, and you puke while you come, and the shame makes you hard all over again, makes you drip. It's one big pity party stocked with therapists and daddies. And it goes on far too long, but there's still some fuel left, still some flesh on the bone.

There's the men looking on as the Doberman obediently tap dances for his blowjob, the circling men who eat thick runny steaks and say, "Yum." There's steam guerillas in torn jackets shooting Russian automatics, and the fleeing glistening rich doing their lopsided swing dance with the poor who, one-handed, slit throats indiscriminately, pearls scattering over steam marble floors. There's round-bellied famine babies and flies. Oh, and there's the fucking therapist again, and storehouses of unused grain guarded by snipers, plus – look who's arrived! It's Julie Andrews from *The Sound of Music.* There's The Slits and Excene, Led Zeppelin and Stravinsky and the reassuring guy from the insurance commercial, all of them writhing around to the war sounds along with a Bosch owl in its flowery eggshell costume dancing on four human legs.

There's close-ups crackling/dripping. Too many cocks to count, bobbing from long green stalks. Assholes wide enough to crawl into, perform mystical rituals there; assholes thick with oracles, competing prophesies echoing up the bowels. And clits with frantic gold wings, clits to trip over, clits that block the sun and the rain, clits with penises growing off them and cuntholes boring into them. Fleshy steam tits and mouths and boots and pink ribbons, and hairdos of television moms with their red-faced cookie-tray innuendoes and cocksucking husbands, there's shit and the common exhortation for Mommy. Fists are shaken at the enemy in triumph, tears shed for Bambi – real tears – plus the excellent come-hither slap.

Masks and props zip around from limb to limb, combusting, damp, bursting into a cloud too heavy with significance to hold its form.

Then it rains and the ash clings to everything.

A little birdcall echoes, lonely pan flute of the guilty. A pussy farts, a tongue recoils. The yeses and noes drop like seed and bounce.

In this soundless afterward, nothing quivers, nothing yawns. There's no one unmaimed to measure the damage and tally the score, so the war ends in a draw.

Both sides have been transfigured beyond recognition, and that seems good enough. The war judges sign off, return to their game of horseshoes in the same cave they use to escape the bomb and the IRS. Who cares who wins, now that the money's been made?

Like clockwork, new moisture, all dirty, gathers on the tip of a high heavy bough. The droplet reflects the first star.

All those parents and wish-figures, all those television nuns and 1970s pool boys just keep mixing together and falling to the forest floor like husks, like so much unloved puppet mulch confetti. By morning all the mental formations will begin fermenting, keeping the roots of surviving foliage moist and hidden. Layers of soft ash will entirely cover the forest floor, then tentative footprints, eyes, hundreds of thousands of blinking eyes, the smell of old smoke and everyday fear. Applause applause applause.

Sweet The Sleep of Heart to Heart

Inanna opened the door for him
Inside the house she shone before him
Like the light of the moon.

Dumuzi looked at her joyously.
He pressed his neck close to hers.
He kissed her.

Though strangers there at the doorway, in her mind she'd fucked him every morning and every evening for nine days in her bed, hands on her belly and thighs, imagining what her skin would feel like shaped by the stranger's hands.

Would the shiver come to him or her first, would it fly between them like echolocation, looping, sewing them together subatomically, at the level of sound? The way every intended touch transforms the body, both bodies, forever? What wonders would their bodies become?

Barely remembering his face or the shape of his hands, just the depth in his eyes and the feeling he brought to her skin as he stood near her, for nine mornings and nights Inanna had seduced her lover in words, not out loud, not written, but words to him in her mind, to herself, sucking her own fingertips.

She would offer her song of seduction both to her lover Dumuzi, and to an audience of eternity to hear, to know her ardor, be its witness, and repeat the phrases, dividing it between their mouths like the cells of an enormous entity, alive, made of words.

What I tell you,
Let the singer weave into song.
What I tell you,
Let it flow from ear to mouth,
Let it pass from old to young.

What she said passed like sticky golden dust, the fierce desire of the simple language blown outward like dandelion feathers, wished-for, sung, more than language. A whole new way of worship, of fucking the earth like it was the holy rockstar of the universe, all suck and sway, with its ass in the air and its full, filthy mouth saying, "Come."

Allowing the courtship to unfold in command and response, tense and slow, gluttonous with metaphor, here is what the Sumerians sang each year at planting time:

Inanna:

My cunt, a shocking emptiness, a rift in heaven, it's flashing and revving like the engine that lights up the moon. My untouched skin is eager, ungalvanized, rising up in lightning rods. Gather your tender unruly forces, your crushing white currents. Fill me with brightness and wind like at the beginning of the world, split my atoms into defiant gleeful storms, make my hips the wild-eyed creatures of your hands, snorting, galloping toward the highest hill.

Who has the courage to hurl himself, arms wide, into my twitching empty sky?" Who will fill me with light, catastrophic, alive?

Dumuzi the Shepherd King replied simply:

Great Lady, I will hurl myself, arms wide into your twitching empty sky. I, Dumuzi, will fill you with light, catastrophic, alive.

He meant:

I will fuck you into abstraction more unstable than light, right now, because I want to.
I will spin you like a newly dying star.
I will make your flesh a forest and feed it to you leaf by leaf and fill your nipples with haunting owls.
I will fuck you because I want to.
I will turn you into a universe made of nothing and intention.
I will make your asshole into a palace with 99 bells clanging against each of its 99 doors.
I will trip your body's most elaborate alarm.
I will split you into all the selves you ever were and all the ones you could have been, and I will kiss their temples.
Then, I will cup you in my hands and tuck you into a tidy spiral.
I will rub sweet cream and crushed poppy petals into your scalp, your belly, the base of your throat, the backs of your thighs, and the soles of your feet.
And because I want to, I will drop you, exhausted, into my mouth and suck you clean.
You will sleep there on my tongue, languageless and warm and known, and I will taste you while I dream of tasting you.

Anna Joy Springer

"Do it now," she said, "Man of my heart," and she meant it. Before he had even touched her.

His body filled, pulsing like hers, and she watched them both change shape: His prick a rising cedar tree, his chest a luxurious garden. Inanna spread into a cool black pool dotted in stars, her cunt a lakeside orchard with overripe figs splashing against the ground like an old man's tears.

Between the two lovers, there in their bed, stretched a clear deep river glinting with fish scales. A cloud of swallows dove erratically, inverting the gray-blue sky. It was in that interstice the lovers met, and where they met themselves.

Hello? Hello.

A shiver and pause, then the sharp crack of thunder. Then a blood-warm downpour and the smell of ozone, audacious and green.

In the Official Version of *The Courtship of Inanna and Dumuzi* what Inanna said was this:

> *My eager impetuous caresser of the navel,*
> *My caresser of the soft thighs,*
> *He is the one my womb loves best,*
> *He is lettuce planted by the water.*

And Dumuzi responded:

> *Water flows on high for your servant.*
> *Bread flows from on high for your servant.*
> *Pour it out for me, Inanna.*

I will drink all you offer.

And in the Official Version, their ancient poem of seduction ends:

> *Sweet is the sleep of hand-to-hand.*
> *Sweeter still the sleep of heart-to-heart.*

Inanna, swollen with brightness, pressed her chest into Dumuzi's back and slept. Outside their window a world of wild beings uncurled new petals and limbs.

April 29, 2006

Dear Winky,

In my classes at Alternative, I met plenty of older feminists who loved bulging pregnant goddesses as proof of a past where women were respected, mothering revered, and peace therefore kept. A past long before Jesus, Muhammad, Moses, or even Zeus.

Plenty of lesbians seemed to find some comfort in swirly-bellied goddesses full of nurturing. They borrowed from cultures they may or may not have had any experience with, looking for a cozy cave, somewhere in storyland, an idyllic lost forest of flesh-covered wombs stocked with poppyseed bagels.

You could find images of fruit-bearing uber-mommies painted

Inanna spoke:

Winky — I'm putting this here so you can know it's real. It's from the "Courtship of Inanna + Dumuzi"

"What I tell you
Let the siger weave into song.
What I tell you,
Let it flow from ear to mouth,
Let it pass from old to young:

My vulva, the horn,
The Boat of Heaven,
Is full of eagerness like the young moon.
My untilled land lies fallow.

As for me, Inanna,
Who will plow my vulva?
Who will plow my high field?
Who will plow my wet ground?

As for me, the young woman,
Who will plow my vulva?
Who will station the ox there?
Who will plow my vulva?"

Dumuzi replied:

"Great Lady, the king will plow your vulva.
I, Dumuzi the King, will plow your vulva."

Inanna:

"Then plow my vulva, man of my heart!

5000 years ago in antiquity, they were writing "Plow my vulva!" Vulva! Gross! Yeay!!!

on murals all over the Mission District. With these reclaimed feminist goddesses, you had to overlook the fact that they were often headless, and their exposed wombs expelled ears of corn, toe-sucking babies and/or planets falling down purple ribbons that snaked up into the stars and down into fields.

These goddess images appeared large as school busses, painted on the sides of buildings in bright parrot colors. Or, on calendars, they danced hand-in-hand, chubby nymphs barefoot in something gossamer. These goddesses glowed with pointy shards of light.

People who liked them did not like perfume, neon light or punk rock; that was the rule. People who liked these motherly archetypes wore multiple shades of purple and seemed constantly annoyed. Some of them went to my college, and some of them taught there. I liked purple fine, but I didn't trust them – the whole undifferentiated glob my mind made of them.

There were so many them-globs in the world, and hardly any were "us," maybe none. Maybe it was just me. "Us" was unique and alone, while "Them" was bonded and bound. That's what I knew for certain at twenty-years-old.

So, I figured that people who liked images of super-fertile giant womb goddesses, birthing waterfalls or planets would find me repulsive and leave me to drown if I fell face down in my puke with my greedy red ass in the air.

Which could happen at any moment.

But there were also a few pissed off second-wavers who were into the scary crazy goddesses, the extreme unpredictable ones. Ones who ripped the skulls off egotistical male demons and ate babies. Criminal goddesses with flaws. Not pretty round headless incubators. Not Mary Mother of her Father's Son. Not the slim-ankled consorts or the ones birthing yams, but the ones who threw fits. Got hysterical, or whatever, fucked up. Banished their dumb boyfriends to hell. Swallowed annoying children.

These rare types of feminists were practically punk in their deep suspicion of virtue. These women were arguers, thorns. Maybe they drank a little. Maybe they had their own kids.

This type of feminist goddess-lover found her mythical role-models in ancient traditions stolen from all around the world, which she pillaged ruthlessly and retranslated for her own purposes.

These ones were guilty, and so were the goddesses they named themselves after. They were not Good. They didn't want some dumbass fairy goddess bullshit, but something you could sink your teeth into and come back bloody.

In the early nineties, representations of these unsoothing deities were harder to find, even in the Mission District.

Good thing I didn't know what I was up to, looking for hope in alternative idols, like a fucking Deadhead walking around saying, "It's a miracle, Sister-Bear."

Or possibly worse: hopeful like all the Anne Geddes-loving WWF-cheering, Gap-shopping yesmen and sorrywomen with their "Hang in There, Baby" kitten posters. Like all those heavy-lidded assholes bulldozing one another cluelessly to the *Chariots of Fire* soundtrack, glory glinting of their dead eyeballs as they tried to outmaneuver each other, not knowing shit, but hopeful, ever hopeful.

I had to go pretty far into hell before I could buy into that shit. I guess that's what hope's for, the totally fucked. Which means a whole lot of people with big-eye puppy calendars are pretty miserable.

So my point is, try not to be a jerk to the hopeful when you meet them in public services offices. They're just as bummed and lost as you are, and lots of them don't even know it.

Ever hopeful,
Nina

Excerpt from Enheduana's Hymn to Inanna

To run, to escape, to quiet and to pacify are yours, Inanna. To rove around, to rush, to rise up, to fall....are yours, Inanna. To open up roads and paths, a place of peace for the journey, a companion for the weak, [a small toy in the gutter] are yours, Inanna.

To turn a man into a woman and a woman into a man are yours, Inanna. Desirability and arousal, goods and property are yours, Inanna. Gain, profit, [tuition, rent, tips, bus fare], great wealth and greater wealth are yours, Inanna.

Assigning virility, dignity, guardian angels, protective deities [even worthless foil creatures and recycled goddesses] and cult centres are yours, Inanna.

Illnesses [including AIDS and terrible addiction, codependency, depression, mania, schizophrenia, dissociation, all identity disorders, and suicide] are yours, Inanna.

To have a wife, [or a girlfriend or teacher, to love, to learn to love, to regret not having loved better, and to try to love with equanimity] are yours, Inanna.

Untruthful words, abuse, to speak inimically and to overstate [to mix truth and fiction without certainty about which is untrue] are yours, Inanna.

The false or true response, the sneer, to commit violence, to extend derision, to speak with hostility, to cause smiling and to be humbled or important, misfortune, hardship, grief, to make happy, to clarify and to darken, agitation, terror, fear, splendour and great awesomeness in radiance, triumph, pursuit... sleeplessness and restlessness, submission, gifts, [fashionable sadomasochism] and [non-monogamy], howling, strife, chaos, opposition, fighting and carnage, [passive-aggressive power struggles], to know everything, to subdue the hostile enemy... are yours, Inanna.

The
ABSOLUTE
Promises of
Synopology

Enron Scabbard

In order to successfully participate in the Here-and-Now Zone, you must learn to be a Jargon-Juggler. Good Jargon-Jugglers use signs strategically. Signs are vehicles of strategy. A good Jargon-Juggler never believes the signs but understands the metaphysical energies of signs.

Signs are energy. If you do not learn to harness the energy of signs, they will control you. They will make you experience physical and mental suffering because of false beliefs. They will make you feel pity, remorse, love, shame, sorrow and despair. They have the power to change your very physiology, to speed your heart rate, alter neurochemistry, and cause dangerous fits of emotionalism.

On your own, you cannot control these energies. Synopology will allow you to transform signs into strategic vehicles without falling victim to belief. But you must begin at the beginning. You will start by following the instructions precisely as outlined in The Synlines I, II, and III, with a qualified Syn-editor.

Here are but a few of the Absolute Promises of Synopology:

- Synopology spells success in sexual relationships. The object of your affection will offer you whatever you want, whether it is more stimulation, less interference, or more support. The object of your affection will believe it is his/her idea to give you more of what you want and will feel guilty when they do not succeed in giving it to you.

- Synopology will allow you to negotiate business deals and other Subtle Wars to your benefit and advancement.

- Your children will no longer seek discursive dominance by "crying" or other manipulative behaviors.

- After training you to control your own physiology with sign-control, Synopology will cause all your Unhealths to disappear entirely without medical invasions or pharmaceutical half-cures. Bones will mend themselves at your command. Kidney stones will be revealed to be nothing more than calcified beliefs.

- Correct application of Synopology strategies will undermine even deadly illnesses such as cancer, diabetes and AIDS. You will never be burdened by addiction or any so-called psychological or "identity" disorder. You will know exactly who you are.

- At later stages of training, you will be able to make yourself invisible, to put thoughts into people's minds from a distance, to avoid all negative and false "emotions," and to manifest the objects of your will.

- With continued practice, you will overcome the False Concept of death itself.

- These are not extravagant promises. They will come to you if you are willing give the Synopology method everything you've got.

June 7, 2006

Dear Winky,

We seek extreme and multiple intensities because we're all crammed so far up our own alienated ego-saturated asses that only a bolt of lightning or a fist can pull us out. Only a cutting, a beating. Pure glee. Something shocking to bring us to life.

It's a truism that sex and violence are interrelated. The bursts of fluid like a star-spangled parade, the kiss like biting a too-cold plum.

It is easier to acknowledge the open-enededness of the self in extreme dissolution. Two come together, force open the skin, the mouths twist, the voices echo, force withstood and the loss of strength that turns a body into a poof of air – these are things done by lust and combat, and their combined forms. Both the healing and killing kinds.

I want you to understand there's a big difference between the healing and killing kinds.

I mean there's supposed to be, if there's any such thing as informed consent. Because how can you be informed before you've experienced the results of your choice, in this moment, in this space? How can you consent to losing the self that consents?

Martin Buber wrote, "We live in the interstices between I and Thou." In other words, I am made by contact, our combined context. Words slam in and fall out, like flesh without cells, but they also transform the flesh of the cells. Every exchange creates a new creature. That's why we hide away in our alienated ego-caves. Who can handle being new to herself all the time?

Where does the body end and ideas begin? At the edges of the skin? Language is as much a part of me as my finger is. Language is made of chemicals and electricity in my nervous system. Every idea, contrived or received, alters the body.

Like how we're making you right now, Winky. Your being is made of tinfoil and spray paint and everything you learn.

Sleep well,
Nina

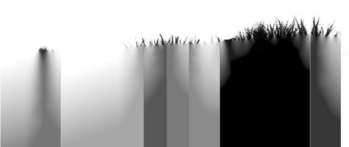

"Strong desire to dissolve persona in an ocean of grace.

A Wind-Up Penis Wobbles In And Out

"I want to fuck you so bad." I said to [Gil]. We'd been girlfriends a couple of weeks.

[Gil] looked suspicious. "You want to fuck me?"

I climbed onto her, putting her hand up under my dress and pulling my panties out of the way. I pushed her onto her back. She moved her knuckles over my clit, down my cunt. I bent forward and bit her bottom lip. I pushed on her hand, took some of it in.

I leaned close to her face and said, "I'm going to fuck you so hard."

She pushed me back a little, squinting, almost whispering, "Are you going to fuck me with your cock?"

It was abrupt, my halt, the look on my face.

Her fingers fell away, limp and reeking. She squeezed her arm out from under my weight, suspicious.

"With my what?" I asked.

"Forget it," she said. She wiped her hand on the futon.

"Why do we have to bring penises into this all of a sudden?" I asked.

She tapped the butt end of a Camel Wide against the floor as if she were killing ants. "I said, forget it. Whatever."

I lit a match and held it up to her face so she'd stop tapping. "I don't understand what's happening right now," I said. "Could you please explain what's going on?"

She squinted and shook her head without lighting her cigarette. The match burned my thumb, and I dropped it onto the bedspread. She reached for her jacket.

"Just because I want us to be women," I said, "which we are, you're going to leave?"

"You're looking at me like I'm the enemy. That's what's going on right now. You're othering me."

"But why did you say that? I'm only telling you I don't understand. Just explain. I thought cocks were the enemy. I thought that was the point. Cocks are what rape. They make monuments of cocks, warheads, Coke bottles. Cocks destroy everything. I'm with you now. We're reclaiming our bodies. I love you for you, just the way you are. Just tell me why you said that."

"I knew this would happen. Of course. A college bisexual. Whatever. If you want to learn, get a book."

She didn't slam my door, she left it open to the hallway. I could hear her boots down the stairwell.

I sat there on my futon, my face warm. My panties were still pulled aside and I felt my crotch, fat and damp, cooling.

My cock?

I wasn't stupid or naive. I'd played dirty games with my boyfriends before. But I'd always been the girl. I thought [Gil] and I had agreed: Men were the force behind everything wrong in the entire world, including capitalism, competition and religion. As lesbians we'd found something beautiful, something completely separate from them. Something pure. One goddamned thing in the world they couldn't stick their dicks in like flags and thereby claim.

I thought she felt the same way. I knew about her father and what he'd done to her. Being a dyke was a political action. Every time we fucked and got off and no penis sprayed its slimy seed, we were winning. We were being revolutionary.

Plus, how could I possibly even pretend I had a cock, the way I looked? I'd be ridiculous. An impossible concept. A world-dominating phallus sticking out from my skirt like a silly sore thumb. And what would I do with one if I had it, me, weapon-wielder, with my swinging double-D's, with my Old World hips and chipped toenail polish?

I had no cock, didn't look like I had a cock, and hated cocks. Not how they felt or looked, but what they meant. What they had come to mean.

I'd thought [Gil] was a dyke, a real one. My first real dyke. Which made me a real dyke, which made me a revolutionary. And she'd said get a book. What kind of book? What was this world I'd woken up in?

THE FOREST OF MYTHOPOESIS

In the Forest of Mythopoesis every thing is our "friend." It has its wants, its limited skills. Having woken up in this forest without provisions, we rely on our Guidebook with its helpful Guidelines for Effective Exchange, which will allow us to "expand our pool of allies" by teaching us to communicate with any "object, material or abstract."

"And everything is," the Guidebook reminds.

We've come to expect a certain style of communication from our friends. We ask that the thunder-cloud speak in "I" statements. Instead, the dark cloud that's been hovering over our heads condenses menacingly.

We respond, "When you express yourself like that, I feel afraid. I don't know what you mean."

The thunder-cloud takes the form of a giant bird, with feathers black as pupils and shiny as water on top of white sand.

Our Guidebook reminds us that not all our friends speak in words. Confident now, we say, "Maybe you could draw a picture of what you need."

And the giant scary raven opens its wings and blocks out the sun entirely. We ask for clarification. We feel frustrated. We turn to "Feelings, Frustration" in the index. We find the page.

It reads, "Be patient. Everything has a story to tell, but it's up to you to learn how to read."

The forest goes dark as a cave, and the rain pummels down upon us.

We are scared. We want to go home. We are failing. We'd like to do it right. We want connection, we've always been so alone. We have no guide, just a secondhand Guidebook. It's from the early 1980s. We're trying our best to understand.

Our mouths fill with water as we plead for clarification. The bird or cloud or violent rain enters our hair, our sweaters, our boots. It touches our skin.

We consult our Guidelines and say slowly and patiently, "I'm not saying that my way of talking is right and yours is wrong. I'm just saying I'd like to be able to hear you, and when you accuse me like that I shut down."

We are craving a kind of lasting union we know we will not experience, because it's fake or happens only after death. But we have become crafty in our isolation, we have read the Guidebook thoroughly, we try the emergency strategy of splitting ourselves into a party of two or more and communicating our needs effectively among ourselves.

We say, "The cloud-friend was full of rage," or, "It wanted release."

We feel ridiculous with our Guidelines turning to pulp and running through our fingers like pudding. We find ourselves flinching, taken unaware by the slap of thunder, the leaping shadow, the sudden root that trips us. We fall hands-first into blackberry bushes, and our hands come back redly yelling at us. They've joined the forest in its strange way of speaking. Our own bodies are turning against us.

We hold our hands up to the sky. We shout, "I respect you. I want to meet you, friend, my friend the enemy, my beloved, I want only that you see me and care."

The rain that's not even wet blinds and deafens us. Our smoldering hands fill with cool black feathers. The throbbing in our palms subsides. We put our fingers in our mouths, and with our mouths full of fingers and rainfeathers, say, "Okay, I think I understand what you mean."

But there's no way to be sure.

We have learned that phenomena enacts itself unpredictably in the Forest of Mythopoesis.

We believe we have learned how to read.

We wonder how to transmit this wisdom to our friends everywhere. We feel driven to tell everyone what we've learned. At the very least someone should update the Guidebook with its out-of-date Guidelines for Effective Exchange.

The rain cloud abandons us; out comes the sun. With our mascara running and our wool tights soaked, we feel lost, again, there together, alone.

We mouth, "Thou," biting into green bark.

May 19, 2006

Dear Winky,

The Goddess is Scary on purpose. She knows the connection between fear of oblivion and yearning for oblivion. In this way she is not only scary but comforting at the same time.

Which is really scary.

So why had I never heard of Inanna or the other goddesses all over the world? Why hadn't the school psychologist back in Junior High told me about badass female archetypes? Why hadn't my mother? Or some book?

Nobody knew they existed, is why. Their stories had been replaced by Literature. Replaced with Prufrock and Captain Caveman. Something more subtle, refined. Maybe erased methodically, through a tricky misogynist conspiracy. Probably not. Probably through something as seemingly innocuous as "taste" and "universality". You know, aesthetics, which are supposedly so neutral. Either way.

Winky, I wasn't looking for role models in manufactured deities, even though that's what it seems like I'm saying.

I was looking for proof that women hadn't ALWAYS been whittled down to natural-born sidekicks.

I needed to know that some people somewhere, at some time, thought of us as multidimensional, which included being powertripping jerks who lost our cool sometimes. Not all the time or never, but sometimes.

I wasn't looking for a figurine to hold in my pocket and rub. I was looking for a possibility of another world, a possibility that the right story, told in the right way, could change everything. And living wouldn't have to be so scary all the time.

And now I know the answer.

Love,

Nina

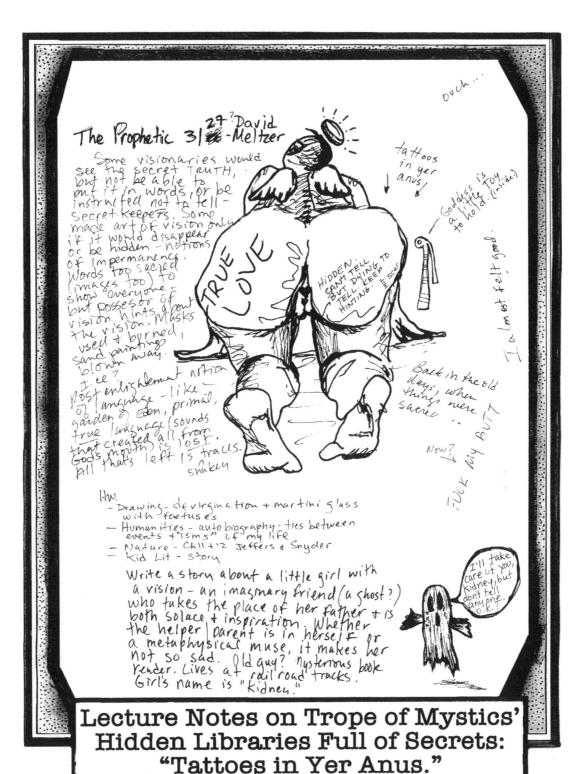

Lecture Notes on Trope of Mystics'
Hidden Libraries Full of Secrets:
"Tattoes in Yer Anus."

The Dualist Deal

In the spring of 1992 [Gil] at least tried to be patient with Blinky who couldn't understand the concepts that she'd inadvertently retained from her early Synopology training.

"Okay, I'll explain it a different way so you can understand. Language and other codes act as crowd control, separating girls from boys and mandating our legibility. I'm a dyke and you're a fetish object. That means we've got some work to do if we want to register in the world, but also there's fun to be had. Are you following?"

[Gil] took on a teacher role with him in a way she wouldn't with me. She didn't tell him to get a book. For whatever reason, I threatened her, and he didn't.

"A veritable lexicon of womanishness or mannishness attaches itself at the groin, then wraps itself up in wily metaphor, using circular reasoning and seductive but slapstick rhetoric encoded in various social laws. Let's say I'm "Small Change." My "own .38" is my "vagina," that for me means my implied "dick," which is a symbol of something else, even, but who cares what, let's stop at dick. It's not there. So it's "missing." It's a lacuna, and can therefore be interpreted all over the place. Get it?"

Blinky blinked.

"All I'm saying, Blinky, is that I'm not a woman and I'm not a man. So, no matter what I do, I lose. But I want my loss to count. I mean, I want to go down with a ten-gun salute. But what if, for instance, I wanted to be the simple victim for a change? Just for a rest. This is America, right? We're all free to want what we want and to go for it. I'm talking dialectics here, remember? You already learned about that last night. So, let's say I wanted to be the innocent, what would that would make you? I mean, relative to me?"

Dualistic reasoning was a tricky and absurd hindrance, popular in this new world. But it seemed to make for good plot.

If [Gil] craved a sense of noble freedom, she'd have to find a way to code as sidekick instead of hero. Switch hats. She'd act out her heroic maneuvers to protect the charismatic hero, shielding him. Inevitably becoming wounded in the act. Then she'd swirl around a few times and die in a triumphant heap, to the glory of the hero and his country.

The neighbors would come and lay expensive flowers on her stoop. Strangers would. "What a Saint [Gil] was," they'd say. "So patient. What a good wife and mother. How brave." They'd pray to images of her, stocky statues with infant proportions and bulging eyes.

Or, the less ostentatious alternative: After taking the bullet, her body would lay undiscovered in a yellow field, and only the mice would know her sacrifice. The mice and the hero. Who could blame him for keeping his mouth shut about what had gone down in battle when she'd shielded him and taken his fatal blow? He wasn't known for eloquent speeches. And there [Gil] would lay, decomposing, shaded by tufted grasses, solitary and honorable in her quiet usefulness.

But only if she were the sidekick, the girl. For that, she needed to find a willing hero.

The dogs were barking, but the phone was not ringing.

Again and Again, Forever

Before [Gil], sex had started feeling like being lonely in a crowd of drunks, then pissed on from a balcony. And even that was an accident.

My body was disgusting to me, and I wouldn't let the men who fucked me see it. They didn't care. They were looking at themselves. I told them to look at themselves.

It wasn't the sexwork; it was what allowed me to do the sexwork, a kind of mind-body split or a split heart. I made a twin of myself and used it as bait so I could be swallowed entirely.

How skillfully I sucked them off, how selflessly I licked their assholes and told them to hold down my arms and fuck me harder, faster, and slap my face, hit me so hard I'd see white. Look at themselves.

It's not that I didn't feel a certain tenderness toward the sweet boys in their afterglow, limp like dead Jesuses, slack with shining eyes, empty of violence. But I didn't think much of these creatures, all wrapped up in their little man-worlds, not knowing anything about mine, not even knowing mine existed. They were predictable, simple. Lazy even. A little undivided attention, a little bravado and criticism, and they'd smell up my room for a week. Then I'd dodge phone calls and avoid certain streets.

True, I picked losers, but the nice vegan copyshop boys wouldn't have me. I wasn't their type. Wounded bisexual liars who lived in halfway houses reached toward me with sticky fingers.

And no way did girls want me. Nobody took me for a dyke with my vintage dresses and long green hair. I was done with sex.

But then I found [Gil]. After we kissed – her mouth pulling my lips like they were nipples – after she pushed me open so wide I bled a smeary ring around her wrist, after I hiccuped sobs and dug trails in the paint on her wall and slammed my fists down against her back, and after I felt like a muscular black-winged horse had flown out from between my thighs then burst open like a star, after she held my shuddering, transformed body, she told me I was hers.

And so I was.

Without thinking to ask, I figured that she was mine, too. That we were each other's.

My First Love Breakup Poem

Love was antithetical and so hatred disguised as love heavied the air and she was playing strategy games she was playing nothing hurts it was so obvious I'm so tired of this war I just wanna take off this uniform and sleep the sleep of peace but there are maps being spread across the bunker floor there are long digressions about the difference between us and them the Bleach Blond tacks pleats in the girls nylon skirt the Brunette boy sits in his boxers and drinks whiskey I roll cigarettes I draw three figures on the inside of the closet door I am dreaming of dreaming I am hearing the white noise the static of privates holed up in a bunker I'm thinking how stir crazy we all are and how conversations are made of deception the girl is trying to hypnotize my comrade they both flick their ashes missing the ashtray with some honed precision a beer spills and I hear all the possible night maneuvers being considered X she says yeah X yeah hey can we hook up with some acid yeah acid they all say no heroin no jim beam no jack daniels remember that vodka remember that crack let's go somewhere and do something then I'm thinking of privates on leave roaming the city obliterated and hailing the coming revolution... everyone is slumped over but strategy games go on forever I am silent but silence means different things in different cultures and so it is not the same silence as the belgian boy in his boxers drinking whiskey he doesn't say anything only the girl was saying anything and only my chessmate was listening she was experiencing the symptoms so common among the ranks the bunker was hers the spanish boy was hers the bleach blond was hers the hypnotized comrade was hers I wasn't thinking at all about lieutenants or generals I was thinking about how this war drags on forever and makes us all so edgy I was remembering the nights of shore leave and the enlisted all blacked out there was no oxygen only smoke my contacts were turning into fingernails there was some minor coup attempt the girl accused me of making faces in her bunker in front of the belgians I said you weren't even looking at me you were hypnotizing my comrade no no I saw you for one split second and you were making faces at me in my bunker in front of the belgians it was strategy but I hadn't considered the game I got my chess set and went searching for oxygen I could hear her screaming Enemy Other Bitch all the way home The War is endless and so now she belongs solely to her bunker I remove my uniform I drink bushmills and swallow belladonna I scratch her name off the We list She writes my name on the They list."

September 21, 1992

God, [Gil] is so paranoid and narcissistic, she acts like everything is this big battle all the time, which, if it is, then it isn't really a very good one if the people fighting don't even know they're fighting.

And she totally was giving me weird looks this afternoon, was obviously pissed that she wasn't the center of attention because she's used to everyone thinking she's so smart and funny wherever she goes. She was pouting in the corner, scratching Greek symbols into the paint of my closet door, and all I did was tell her to stop it and she freaked out.

And now she's pissed because I can't go over there tonight. She said that I am playing power games with her. But I have to read for my Erotic Poetry paper on Inanna.

She's like, "You're always sooo busy." Like I'm lying and have a whole secret life, like another girlfriend or something instead of two jobs, two bands and full-time school.

She gets really mad – it's intense.

But then, I feel bad, like maybe I'm not spending enough time over there with her. But I spent three nights there already this week! She should understand that I'm trying to get my shit together to get out of this fucked-up country. I don't care about Clinton and all his promises. He's a benign smiling self-seeking wannabe patriarch, which may be even worse than being an outright disgusting creep like Bush. I want to move someplace where everyone gets to go to the doctor when they're hurt and everyone gets to go to school and where the people think art is important.

I can't help it that I have more interesting things to do than put my whole life into a relationship like some wifey-wife from the 1950s.

And I'm pretty sure I didn't do anything to deserve this shit she's throwing at me about playing power games. I've been pretty clear about my priorities. I'm trying to LEARN. If I'm not LEARNING I might as well KILL myself right now because that's the WHOLE POINT of life if there is any point.

P.S.!!! Did she really break up with me with a TYPED POEM?

Anna Joy Springer

Power Games

Ishtar spies proud Gilgamesh who's just killed Humbaba in the cedar forest and brought back the load of cedar logs he's pillaged for her temple. He's so fine that Ishtar gawks. His hair is wet, and curls cling to his neck, salty against his collarbone. His hands are rough and thick.

Ishtar calls out,

> Come, Gilgamesh, be you my bridegroom! Grant me your fruits, O grant me! Be you my husband and I your wife!"

Still overproud and excited, he answers,

> [Who is there] would take you in marriage? [You, a frost that congeals no] ice, a louvre-door that stays [not] breeze nor draught, a palace that massacres … warriors, an elephant which … its hoods, bitumen that [stains the hands] of its bearer, limestone that [weakens] a wall of ashlar, a battering ram that destroys [the walls of] the enemy, a shoe that bites the foot of its owner! What bridegroom of yours did endure for ever? What brave warrior of yours went up [to the heavens?]

An audience listening to the poem might have identified with headstrong Gilgamesh, but would have pitied him, too. When he made his speech cursing Ishtar the crowd would have cringed, knowing what was coming, having heard the story before: The fierce hero Gilgamesh would follow his will right off a cliff.

The lesson, like the meaning of life, would be simple and direct: There was no way to win a revolt, kings against gods, or slaves against kings. But Gilgamesh, stuck in storyspace outside of time, would be unable to hear the warnings of the audience.

So, he continues insulting Ishtar:

> Come, let me tell [you the tale] of your lovers: Dumuzi, the lover of your youth. Year upon year to lamenting you doomed him …

When she was finished with the allallu-bird and broke his wing, all he could do was cry, "My wing!" She loved the lion, but dug him pits to fall into, and she loved the horse, but domesticated him and forced him to drink dirty water.

Gilgamesh reminds Ishtar of how she turned one poor herdsman into a wolf who was then bitten by his own sheep dogs, and how she transformed her father's gardener into a dwarf.

In the Official Version, Ishtar gets her revenge by sending the Bull of Heaven down to earth to eat everything growing in the fields and drink all the water in the rivers and canals so there will be a terrible famine and drought there in the windy desert.

The Official Version was based largely on the Babylonian rendition. The Baby-lonian Epic came 600 years after the one first written in Sumeria.

There are some important differences between the earlier Sumerian and the later Babylonian epics: In the Sumerian tale, the Goddess Inanna approaches King Bilgames in the shade of the wall where the temple whores recite poetry. She invites him to join her in bed. There he can avoid for awhile his duties of passing judgment and rendering verdicts. Would he marry her?

Bilgames, brave killer of monsters, is afraid. He runs to his mother, the wild cow goddess, to tell her what has happened and ask her advice.

Bilgames' mother, tells him:

> The gifts of Inanna must not enter your chamber, the divine Palace Lady must not weaken your warrior's arm!

Bilgames goes back to the wall and is about to give Inanna his answer to her proposal. But what did he say? There is a long lacuna in the clay tablet, where a whole section of the story has been lost.

Most translators insist that, in the older version, Bilgames simply lists Inanna's betrayals exactly as he does in the later Babylonian Epic. But the truth is, nobody knows what was lost in the erasure. It could have been anything at all.

Ringgggg.

May 28, 2006

Okay, Winky, so maybe I was as crazy as [Gil]. Without the diagnosis. Maybe I still am. Yeah, maybe. Now, I talk to inanimate objects like they're my BFF. No offense.

Now I'm a grown up. I stayed alive and now here I am with a job and health insurance. I have enough security to finally be an anarchist and devote myself to spiritual practice. Now I eat varied whole grains and drink water. I celebrate Thanksgiving, I try to have long-term relationships with women, and I often brush my teeth.

Now I am here, trying to be here. Where did that person I was before go? I really liked her. Is there a forest for her somewhere, and are you there with her, Winky? I don't want her to have to have died so I could be here to tell about her zany adventures before she went straight. And which fucker in the future is choking me out, so that she can claim dibs on the next installment?

[Gil] had multiple personality disorder, in the language of the day. What did I have? Historical Fictionalization of Selfhood Disorder? Associative Narrativity Disorder? Graphomaniacal Denial Disorder? Mass Suicide-by-Proxy Disorder? What do I have now? Shrinks have decided so-called "dissociative disorders" spread out along a spectrum, and everyone has them in this day and age.

For instance, from time to time everyone goes on autopilot while driving home from work and doesn't remember anything from the 20-minute commute. That's a form of dissociation. Or if you start reading all the shop signs aloud when you're driving through the city, and you keep reading them without even realizing you're doing it, that's a form of dissociation. There are all sorts of levels of checking out. You don't have to be a total puppet-show Sybil to be multiple anymore. Now, you can just be postmodern. Or a worker-consumer. Or just trying to live without causing harm. Try that. Try finding something to wear and something to eat.

So the point, Winky, is this: Just remember when you get to the City, you might feel a little beside yourself. But I'm letting you know that it's normal to fall apart in transition. They say moving is very stressful.

Anyway, to answer your anticipated question, a few days after the "coup," when [Gil] broke up with me, we saw each other below my apartment in front of the Walgreens at the corner of Haight and Filmore. She was waiting at the bus stop for the No. 22. Just seeing her weird smirky face made me laugh. She laughed, too. She opened her arms, and I went to her. So then I was her girlfriend again, just like that.

I remember standing apart from myself, watching myself go back to her, watching myself move toward certain danger, not caring, going toward it anyway like the skinny heroine in a monster movie that you want to shout to: "Don't go back into the house!" But you know she has to because the movie's only half-over, so your dread is mixed with a little excitement about what's going to happen next because you pretty much already know how the story will end.

And you know there'll be a sequel.

– Nina

Ruling Class Poetics

King Sargon's storytellers began entertaining audiences with tales of Ishtar's adventures, which she always won fabulously. They flooded the entertainment zones with Ishtar's heroics

No longer a fleshy fertility goddess, she evolved into a Hollywood-style fucking and killing machine. Sargon's storytellers merged her with the Goddess Inanna so she'd be recognizable to his new subjects.

In the new cultural lexicon, love became cross-referenced with war, and by extension, sex overlapped with crimes of passion, state sanctioned murder and torture. Victory slipped into the skin of longing.

The confusion was numbing at first, pacifying like a special gas or tea. Over time, however, Sargon's ingenious goddess-merging began to rewire the discursive circuitry so that love seemed both horrifying and blissful, and so did war.

Everything got all fucked up, all mixed up in everybody's heads. Rape became a word, then, for an effective war strategy. And because of mass rape the women coated their assholes and cunts in animal dung, as one line of defense to disgust their invaders.

So the next invaders called the women filthy, which caused the women shame, and after raping them while holding their noses the invaders hosed them down and married them out of pity mixed with ambition – for the women could work and breed workers, which was probably better for everyone than letting the women die in their shivering soup.

So, marriage, slavery, rape, war, pity, love, disgust, shame and redemption lodged themselves in a snarl in their sons' and daughters' brains.

Again, this is right about the same moment when authorship begins, poetry chiseled and signed.

September 25, 1992

[Gil]'s not mad at me anymore. I'm here in her room. She's in the kitchen talking to her roommate about something – the rent, his late night speed-dealing – I don't know.

Last time I was here she kept saying we should be safe, so I bought some rubber gloves that go up to the elbow. They're black and hot, not like the medical ones in a box – yuck.

I hate authority figures, especially doctors. I don't understand why anyone would find regular latex gloves sexy. They're trying to make latex seem like a big aphrodisiac in all these bus shelter ads, and now they're trying to make it so that guys have to wear condoms in porno movies, which they should, but it's about as sexy as going to the gynecologist or the dentist.

I like the long black gloves; they feel really good. But at the same time I feel like a sell-out, because all that leather and rubber stuff at the store seems so obvious. Plus, it's so expensive; it's like a status symbol if you have a whole outfit. It's like pretending to be tough when you're really just dressing up in expensive clothes. And it's like everything rich people do. They dress up in leather because they have no imagination, they pay to have their fantasies created for them. I hate obviousness. It's disgusting that you have to prove who you are by what you buy, not what you make.

It's all about the outfit and what it makes you mean to others. You're pretending to mean one thing, "I'm into danger and creativity," but really you mean, "I'm rich and like to seem wild." Both of those things together is what you code for, and both of those things – your intention and your projected false intention – is what you mean. Which probably gets you laid because you're rich.

(Why do rich people have such tight pores? Is it that their rich ancestors never had to grow big pores to let out all the sweat? Why don't they have insane cellulite and bunions? Why do they get to be rich AND pretty AND get laid whenever they want? Are they so boring and complacent because they're so satisfied with themselves?)

I don't want my fantasies pre-made for me. I want to be wrapped up like a mummy in wide pink satin ribbons and have my lover tell me about how all the punk-rock fairies are flying around me trying

to find an opening in my cocoon, so they can all lick my nipples like it's a big festival and then fly up inside me and swim through my veins which'd make me come from every part of my body, not just my cunt. You'd never see them sell that in a store.

Why does everyone just think of whips and chains and chaps and nurse outfits, when you could imagine anything? Isn't that few moments of intensified magical freedom what sex is for?

The saddest part about working at the peepshow is realizing how boring people are. They just want something they know. Now I wear Victoria's Secret so I can look less punk and get more customers. Smiling like Miss America. I bought two bra and panty sets and stockings and a white see-through robe with flowers. White! Talk about selling out. But it's kind of pretty. Also I got a new vibrator because that's what makes the real money. Everything came out to over two-hundred dollars, so I'm eating ramen until I make it back, hopefully in two or three days, if it's not too slow.

One thing that's weird is [Gil] makes me take off my makeup and take a shower immediately when I get to her house after work. It's creepy, the way she looks at me. Like I'm dirty. Which seems really hypocritical after everything she's done for money.

My Body Reformed

"Bob" was pinkish-grey, normal penis length, though a little small for my taste. It looked like an actual penis but a little more perfect, sort of young. The book I'd read said to buy silicone. The silicone would warm to body temperature, or after boiling it for hygiene and letting it cool a little, I could use it almost hot.

Bob the penis was ninety dollars.

"And do you need a harness?" the salesgirl asked.

"Yeah, I guess I will probably need a harness. What's the cheapest kind of harness?"

She showed me a limp something made out of backpack material with Velcro attachments. Two choices: lime green or purple.

"Oh," I said. "What's the next cheapest?"

She gave me a strappy flimsy leather thing.

"This is a popular model," she said. It looked popular. Popular and cheap and boring. I didn't like the way any of them looked. Why couldn't they make something pretty for girls? Maybe I could Beadazzle it.

I said I'd take the popular model.

It was sixty dollars. She told me I should try it on before I took it home. I had already left my body. She walked me to the dressing room.

The harness was an impossible puzzle of straps and rings, and I was a sweaty dumbass. After a while, she knocked on the door, startling me. "Do you need some help in there? That one can be hard to figure out at first."

"No that's okay, I got it." If the skinny vibrator co-op salesgirl with pointy glasses and multiple lovers tried to walk in on me like they did in the bra department dressing room, I would start crying.

I pulled the straps snug until my hips choked out, flesh bulging weirdly. It was worse than bathing suit shopping. My thighs and ass were rippled and ugly in the dressing room light. How did people do this? Did you have to be rich AND skinny to be a dyke in San Francisco?

"I'm not here to indoctrinate you," [Gil] had said more than once.

"Why not?" I'd asked. "I'd do it for you if I were the one with experience."

"Read a book," she'd said, "They make them for people like you."

Was [Gil], tough as she was, ashamed of sex, like a regular girl? Was it impossible for her to say what she wanted aloud, blow whatever cover she thought I was into? The daddy, the hero, the hard. I just wanted my initiation. I imagined it like a 1970s movie about a secret devil cult at an all-girl school. There'd be a ceremony in a dank basement with an exchange of solemn words, feathering torches. Some dyke would cut my hand and squeeze the blood into a bowl, then swear on a sacred book. I wanted to be part of something important.

If I would have had a friend, someone I met in "Nature As A Concept" or "The Prophetic" or even someone from the peepshow, I would have brought that friend to the store with me. I might've brought her. That's what normal people do when they're in new territory or scared – they bring a friend; that's the normal response.

But I didn't have a friend. What sort of someone would be there with me in the dressing room, laughing with me as I struggled with the harness. How would such a thing occur? I did things on my own, like my mother and her mother before her. Strong, alienated working-class women, figuring it out and getting it done.

And so, without witness, I found myself twisting weirdly to see as much of my wide bumpy ass as I could in the mirror. I grimaced. I tried to rearrange the straps into a more flattering V. Impossible. Okay, I'd just never let her see my ass. Blindfolds should come free with every harness.

I paid in ones and fives. The counter girl said, "Oh, Bob. People have very nice things to say about Bob." She seemed nice. Maybe she'd be my friend. She handed me a black paper sack with handles, like from the makeup counter at fancy department stores.

I sheepishly took the bag to [Gil]'s apartment. Outside, I called her from the pay phone on the corner and told her, "I have a surprise."

Inside, I lay Bob on the bed between us, then I spread out the harness. [Gil] nuzzled me like a mother baboon, like I'd won the fucking spelling bee. She went coy, sort of humid and lithe.

"Close your eyes," I said. "Keep them closed." I took off all my clothes and fixed the harness in place. I kept checking to see if she was peeking. It took a long time to get everything together. Then I stood there, ridiculous, trying to figure out what pose might look at least a little sexy.

For a femme to let herself intentionally look ugly during sex is a deeply sacrificial act. Not knowing I was a femme, I just thought, "Well, dykes aren't supposed to care about patriarchal standards of beauty."

It had only been a couple weeks since I'd scared her away from my apartment by telling her I didn't want any boys in our bedroom. I had already learned to fuck her as if she were a girl and I was a boy. It was easy. I liked it. I'd talked her through all sorts of heterosexual conquest scenarios.

I'd learned to make a bird-head with my fingers, then curl them into a fist and move my arm like a jackhammer, calling her names. She liked it. I liked it. It was amazing. There were so many secret worlds in the city, better and better ones, hidden behind normal looking doors, and they were real, they were there. All you had to do was find them. They were there.

But even with my fist in her, she'd never been limpid like this. It was the presence of this thing, this penis-shaped thing. My prosthesis was more hers than mine. She made it alive, turned it to flesh, then she took it from me and went all womanly, like from an old movie. She looked beautiful.

I stood facing her. "Okay, you can open your eyes."

On cue they pooled, her pupils expanding like oracle caves. Her eyelids fell heavy, her mouth went full, her breathing changed and I recognized her. It was as if I'd never seen her before.

I knew exactly what her longing felt like, fat and warm with its hundred stretching arms. She was me there on her back on the bed.

I went to her.

I watched myself hook my fingers into her mouth, felt the slice of her lower teeth on them, her tongue. I climbed between her knees pushing them apart easily,

and like my boyfriend used to do, I folded a pillow under her ass to tilt her up. I loved her smell, like some other world, a place to escape to, a humid, fern-covered place.

"Oh my sweet beautiful boy," she said, and I tried to keep calm. I held the tip of the dick and rubbed it slow down the length of her cunt, like a tongue. Pushed into her, just the head, and she gasped. I pulled out.

"Sweet boy, don't be afraid," she said. "I know you've never done this before." She soothed in that tone they call "motherly." I recognized the cue.

But I felt like a man, not a boy.

"Go in," she said.

With my mouth on her ear I said, "You don't tell me. You beg me."

She changed again, from warm and sugar-liquidy to something more focused and sharp. Her eyes latched onto mine. She cupped my cheeks in both hands, her hips rising and falling like breath.

"Please. Please fuck me."

"With what?"

"Please. With your cock."

The magical words: With your cock.

And then I became somebody else. I fucked like I was drinking my first clean water in days. I became my thrust, all movement and nerve.

My cock. There it was. There I was.

I had never known myself at all. There had never been a self to know, just this – this rising and falling, this expanding form where I was lost and didn't care, leading, guiding, wholly sacrificed to her rhythm, her sound.

Only Hibernating

In the Sumerian *Epic of Gilgamesh* tablet where there is a long break in the text, there might never have been any writing at all.

Or Inanna could have said, "I changed my mind. I don't want you to be my Dumuzi."

Gilgamesh might have said, "Okay, I'll marry you, but first we have to get rid of that little shit, Enkidu."

It could have said anything.

Did the words fall to dust? Were they chipped away? Could the missing lines have changed history?

There is another copy of that text, intact, somewhere in a library buried deep in the sand. In fact, there is more than one copy, more than one library.

It's bumper-to-bumper libraries deep underground in the desert north of Basra. They are only sleeping, but likely will never be roused.

Oct 17 - [Gil's]

~~Xgrll~~ being so ~~pretto~~ godbessly sweet to me. She seems to think that this sudden gentleness is due her recent acquisition of a creme-colored strapless bra & panty set from Victoria's Secret. Last night I was torturing myself with her autobiography. ~~XXXXXXXXXXXXX~~

~~XXXXXXXXXXXXXXXXXXXXXXXXXXXXXXXX~~
~~XXXXXXXXXXXXXXXXXXXXXXXXXXXXXXXX~~
~~XXXXXXXXXXXXXXXXXXXXXXXXXXXXXXXX~~
~~XXXXXXXXXXXXXXXXXXXXXXXXXXXXXXXX~~
~~XXXXXXXXXXXXXXXXXXXXXXXXXXXXXXXX~~
~~XXXXXXXXXXXXXXXXXXXXXXXXXXXXXXXX~~
~~XXXXXXXXXXXXXXXXXXXXXXXXXXXXXXXX~~
~~XXXXXXXXXXXXXXXXXXXXXXXXXXXXXXXX~~
~~XXXXXXXXXXXXXXXXXXXXXXXXXXXXXXXX~~
~~XXXXXXXXXXXXXXXXXXXXXXXXXXXXXXXX~~

Nina,

~~& xxxxx~~ Oh ~~XXXXX~~ there's too many [Gil], [Gil], [Gil] things that're opposite. ~~XXXXXXXXXXXXXXXX~~ makes me mad. She's such my favorite person & while yesterday I was so ready to hate myself for holding onto her when

---

I made her into a "girl." It's what she wanted. Not really, but for me to act like she was, for me to be the boy.

Blinky's Revelation

Back in his forest, there was no lesbian vampire schoolgirl genre of literary erotica. No Nazi-themed play parties with vegan hors d'ouvres for a parade of blindered horseys with flowing tails shoved up their behinds, ridden by a cadre of whooping daddies in white tank tops.

Blinky wasn't into all that shit back at home in the forest where sex was not a concept.

In the forest, it felt good to lie in the grass in the sun. To lick oneself. To rub against the bark of a tree. To spray a stream of eggs down into a crevice or mount a hind end. It felt mildly orgasmic to yawn. There were no boundaries or contracts or safe words.

Nobody enjoyed watching a smaller thing stutter and equivocate. Every animal apologized when they hurt another one's feelings, and meant it. Nobody got their wires crossed. It felt good to watch the seasons change, the bodies change, the weather. It felt sexy to see the sun rise out of the trees, to feel it warm their leaves and cast shadows everywhere.

In the forest, back home, everyone ate moss, green leaves, mushrooms and cold water. No one fell in love with the blood or the eyes in their meat. No one ran away or hid. In the forest there was no unconscious power-tripping and there was no boring public art. Everyone was happy there, safe and free.

In the City, Blinky felt the bite of the weather, the cruelty of music. Dogs and cats had desperate eyes, and beautiful women clawed at their skin. Everything seemed backward.

Blinky said to himself, "It's just as I'd dreamed while I was hibernating in my cave."

He said, "Everything I enjoyed and believed was true is gone, including myself as I was in the forest."

Without meaning to, he came, which confused him and hurt. It felt like he'd fucked a live outlet. He was betrayed and hyper-aware of the schism between body and mind, its rough edges.

He blinked and said, "So this is one kind of death, I guess."

June 21, 2006

Dear Winky,

I'd never hit anyone before I hit [Gil while we were playing in bed]. Not even in grade school. I'd never fought back when I was baited or pushed in the chest. I'd never hit my mother.

I knew that my violence wasn't simply a hyper-aggressive or passive-aggressive strategy to win [Gil]'s approval. I wasn't only trying to please her, to serve her; often I wanted to hurt her for real. Or to slap her into my world.

Where had she gone and who was I hitting?

Sometimes, truthfully, I didn't care.

There we were, alone together, slamming our little universes into each other, getting off side by side. Truly brutal, I did not recognize myself.

Finally.

So I learned that dissolution could be achieved through all sorts of violent shake-ups. Starving praying shooting-up bottoming dancing fucking all of them at once reading writing fighting asphyxiation, all of it, killing someone, watching someone cry.

There were many ways to lose yourself in ways that felt divine, to be happily lost in the Metaforest, to feel relief, that almost-remembered state before consciousness, that ecstatic realm of the freshly post-fetal.

I know I'm getting far out here, Winky, I know I sound like a burn-out trying to psycho-babble a teenage girl on mushrooms into his skanky patchouli bed. It's the pitfall of language.

And it's why, no matter how good the Guidebook, you still have to go into the forest yourself. It's that getting lost, the lust for it, all the ways and wrongways you go. All those counterfeit freedoms you will chase down like rabbits.

I'm trying to tell you how fun they will be, until they're not anymore. You'll find yourself thinking that the only lasting way to kill your Self is to kill yourself.

It's a logical conclusion, but too logical to be right. Which is why I'm trying to teach you how to read around logic.

What you need to know is that [Gil] and I were trying, Winky, we were trying in perversion to find a way outside narcissism. We were trying to find a way to believe that a world existed outside of our minds. We needed to short-circuit discourse, but in conversation.

I know that's oxymoronic, or just moronic, but that's what we were getting to. A kind of shared glossolalia, or even a silence that'd be true. A sort of stab at the left-handed path, as some call it, but without formal practice or right understanding.

Still, we were trying in the right direction. Imperfect means, but right impulse. Without a trustworthy guide.

I want you to trust me, Winky.

Sincerely,

Nina

October 28, 1992

It's going to be Halloween soon. I thought I heard a real ghost chuckle a few minutes ago.

I'm sooo high.

I called [Gil] from the phone booth and told her to get ready. I told her the things she needed to get: A mirror, some candles, her big fishing knife. I would bring everything else.

(You stole your roommate's mirror, the fag speed dealer's. Everyone was home. You put on my fishnets like I told you to.)

You: Shaved over the ear, broad shoulders, Betty Davis eyes, used-to-be-butch, black boots, overalls and homeboy hats, smell of Portuguese Breakfast soap and gardenia, erratically clean Virgo scholar, bigmouth, drama queen, book diva, barely 29, thirteen step-ladder scars along the base of your spine – the first colonies or years of torture. A skull-faced jester on your neck with the words "Noble Savage" underneath.

To encounter your inner child is to be raped.

My knife's at your throat and I put your lipstick on you, yank your neck around to make you see what you look like when you're a girl, a little nothing, beggin' for it...

We had sex and she was the most beautiful woman in the world, the wise whore (as all whores are), and me the dumb hermaphroditic girl/boy, and I was jerked off and devirginated by this whore because I was going to learn how to be a boy whore.

I still am unfamiliar with being a boy in a boyish girl's eyes. Platonic Love was really another term for the circle jerk. The look not touch.

How do we, as feminists, silence this violent desire?

WE DON'T! YIPPEE!

She wanted me to put my whole fist up her asshole. I tried and tried, but it wouldn't go in. She seemed happy, anyway. But she was "too turned on to come." Maybe it was the speed. She's getting really skinny.

Honestly she was so beautiful, her body has gotten so light. I could lift up her like she was nothing.

Ringgggg. Rinnngggggg.

Of Course

Wasn't every 20-year-old girl with half a brain looking for the ornate gates of hell? To scrape off the safety-first dust of diet pills and clean panties and Say No To Drugs of our girl-hating culture?

Weren't we all looking for something untamed and untameable to keep in our purses for later? To endanger ourselves, nonstop, to love bitterly, the wrong way, like childhood?

June 23, 2006

Dear Winky,

You know I don't mean it's bad when I call our attempts a kind of creative perversion, right? You know I mean it's a good place to start. Forced dissociation isn't bad, but it's dangerous. It's so easy to get lost and stay there. Or it's easy to find something to believe in and hold onto it and create a whole new system to get stuck in like all those wealthy consciousness shrinks who were sure LSD would save the world. Remember this, Winky, lost and stuck are the City's two main dangers.

We were idealists, me and [Gil]. If you were only logical, we would seem like nihilists. But it's the idealists who commit suicide, not nihilists. That's the big mistake you'd make if you didn't know how to think outside of logic.

Anyway, what I'm getting at is that these instructions are meant to help you without being too dangerous. I don't want to hurt you, Winky. In fact I've sworn off causing harm in general, when I can get away with it. That's the vow anyway. I still kill mosquitoes, pay taxes, and buy new clothes from the mall, but at least I feel terrible about it. So anyway, I've made my choice, and you'll have to make yours. Every day you'll have to. I'm just trying to prepare you.

Love,
Nina

Oct 29, 1992

She read somebody's translation of Homer's poems - we both needed a beating, really bad so I beat her into beating me into beating her. We did all this with one belt end circled around my wrist + one tied around her neck, we might've fallen into a net from a tightrope, dueling, it was that absurd, sharks entangled in tuna lines. I didn't understand when she bent close to my face + said "yer body's sacred to me I love you" that was trickery + I was forced to beat her.

And then we finally went to SLEEP.

She told me my body was sacred (as a way to get me to beat her).

"Victim" As A Metaphor

For Halloween, I had to work at the peepshow. But I wasn't going to be predictable and dress up as a sexy vampire with a long black wig and all the rest – the lips, the teeth, the cobweb gloves. Instead, I'd be the victim. White lace cut down to my sternum, tight across my hips. Two bloody holes fresh on my throat. An invitation.

Nobody came in except maybe a handful of guys. And only one of them wanted my special holiday show. I was too close to home, too scary. Halloween for them was for laughing at fear, not for dropping into it like a bottomless lake.

If I had been a customer, and a peepshow girl was up for playing dead, I'd blow my whole paycheck. I'd stay in her booth for the four-hour shift, telling her the ways she died while she brought her cool white face closer and closer to the glass and watched me feed my twenties into the slot. Her eyes would be tired, her bite marks smeared, and I'd ask her to open her mouth so I could see inside. Touch her dead tongue with my finger. She'd wake up and die again all night with my cock in her, against her, my hands on her throat, my knife in her guts, my thighs sticky with blood.

If I had been a customer, and there'd been a peepshow girl in victim drag, sipping her corner store screwdriver, sadly waiting to be chosen, she's the one I'd pick. So she's the one I was.

I was more than bored, drunk and sad. There was true depth of sorrow in my eyes. I saw them in the reflection of the peepshow glass. My secret? [Gil] had grabbed me by the neck when I'd tried to leave her apartment in the middle of a fight the night before.

Beneath the white powder there were dark bruises on my neck.

Wasn't it funny? Wasn't it a great fucking joke, this private joke of mine, how I'd covered these dark blue marks with victim makeup? For Halloween? To be scary? To laugh?

She had blocked the door and said, "You're sleeping here," and while she guided me back to the bed, she choked me so hard I thought I might really die. I took off my clothes again and, blinking, tried to sleep.

Such a funny irony, the victim girl on Halloween, bruises looking like part of the props. One sort of clown among others, in tight lace smeared with glycerine blood. What to do when it gets too scary: Make it funny, dress it up.

Only one customer came in to see me for more than three minutes. He put in a twenty – twelve minutes. He didn't want me to pick up the phone. He sat on the small round stool and didn't pull closer.

I went through my luring routine, hawking my parts like the hand model on the home shopping channel, framing close-ups for him, just a tease, to find out his interest.

I moved my mouth toward Bob the penis, that sat on the little ledge at the edge of the window separating the customer from me. I licked the dick trying to mesmerize the customer with my tongue, squeezing the base and licking its head like I would the tip of his cock, then running my tongue down the shaft, wetting the whole thing, feeling it fill my mouth, human and needy. I pulled my mouth up and down, lifting my eyes.

Pick the One That Best Represents Your Desire.

If at this point he was still there, I would have him. I would gesture for him to roll his stool closer to the window and undo his fly. While I sucked, he could wet his hand and squeeze his cock, and we'd be together almost.

He was watching my face intently, as I'd planned. But not with the captive, capturing eyes I needed. Not sliding in another twenty. In his stinky little closet, head leaned against the wall, he was crying. Not sobbing. The tears slid thinly down his cheeks, and he made no move to wipe them away.

I pulled my mouth off Bob and pushed myself up to sit cross-legged, facing him.

The customer just sat there and stared at me with soft heartbroken eyes, and the tears, more like oil than saltwater, kept sliding slow and thin, wide trails dripping from his jaw to the cummy floor. It was like he knew. It was like he knew what had happened to me and it hurt him, too.

Or his estranged daughter was a peepshow girl.

Or maybe his daughter had just been killed by her boyfriend, and I looked like her.

Probably he was just a pervert and this was his thing.

He could be a priest.

I watched the man cry, and he let me. I was trying to decide if this was some fetish thing and how I could work it for another twenty, maybe pick up the phone and play mommy therapist baby what's wrong.

I strategized. I watched.

And then, fuck, my eyes welled, too. For no reason.

There we were.

I cried with him for the final six minutes of the show. We faced each other through the glass, knowing, not knowing, not saying a thing.

THE FOREST OF MANDATORY INNOCENCE

Two fine children, hair thin as silk, pink-tongued as lambs, teeth white as clouds, frightened and betrayed by adult romance, set sail into The Forest of Mandatory Innocence. They brought a loaf of crumbs to break off and scatter beneath he ancient oaks with their grabby hands, their old men's hats, their cigar smoke, their jokes about tender young thighs, tastes like chicken.

The oaks watched the kids push open the witch's gate.

The loaf of bread was ruined by rain. The oaks rubbed their limbs, said, "Oh boy," and the rats in the yard chased their tails, sang, "Oh boy oh boy oh boy."

All of nature feeds on loss.

Doesn't it?

It had taken great effort and courage to find the witch's house. The two children entered the meager property that occupied an unexpected clearing in the forest. It looked less like a house than a candy store or a toy store or a circus, but it was none of those.

Of course, of course: The toys had teeth, the candy forced sleep. The tired heroes were scooped from the steps and tucked into their pie-dough bedding. Their heads drooped over pillows of caramelized onion. There was a familiar enactment of the spinster's white up-knotted hair unwound, one hair plucked and split like a zipper, the killing blade so honed. A crow laughing, a pot lid tapping. A crazy old woman with cats in the forest, in the story, the one everyone knows about the Forest of Mandatory Innocence. Everyone knows. We keep sticking the rascals there alone, adorable in their little rags.

Love loves protecting.

So why don't we write the tiny ones into the arms of loving protectors, give them new sneakers, fresh butter, a horse? Why study their fluttering eyelids, wringing our hands?

And why curse that old forest hermit, giving her only babies for meat?

The children spent their young lives being innocent and shivering. In turn, they never became cruel. They sweetened and sweetened. They learned to behave. So hungry, still so well behaved. Nobody knows where they are except us, nobody cares for these cold little ones.

The ticking, the horrible ticking. Why don't we help them?

The toadstools are red. The rapists want dinner. The old woman pulls off her old-woman suit.

The ticking oven timer begins to sound more familiar. The timer goes off.

Oh, that's it. The ringing, it sounds like an old-fashioned phone! Angry. Ringing and ringing, disturbing the neighbors. Ringing and ringing, but where is the phone?

Oh, listen. It's stopped. So peaceful, the silence.

Tuck in your napkin, it's time to eat. Here's your roasted sacrifice, your tender nibble.

Weep now, weep into your hands. Salt your meal with your pure, pure tears, and enjoy your difficulty swallowing.

I will.

Delicious.

Pull up a chair.

What children are for in the forest together our minds have made and remade.

Not Knowing Shit

If we want to stay alive we have to pretend to like our captor, and then, upsettingly, we find things to like about our captor. That kind of shit.

Bliss: Both alone and not alone, unwitnessed and under surveillance. Like in a dream, the hot shame of being naked in class, all the time. We are in danger. It's bigger than institutional, bigger than historical.

Bliss: Not knowing what "it" is.

Bliss: Losing it. And it may be lost for good this time. Finally. Seeing the stage and the props, but not seeing the stagehands' mechanical hands. The green exit sign is there but it's broken.

Bliss: The swirling bulimia toilet bowl of knowing and not knowing.

Bliss: No words to describe it. You know what I mean. Not knowing shit.

It's not a state between ignorance and wisdom. Like grief, there's no way to trick it.

Bliss: But we don't know that yet.

We are going to make it feel okay, even rad, amazing, this sense of vertigo.

This falling into cruel, self-centered adulthood.

August 15, 2006

Winky,

    This afternoon while you were napping, I heard on the radio that all these archaeologists are freaking out about the loss of so many ancient Babylonian objects because of the wars. Among the missing irreplaceables is an image of Inanna pressed into clay, flanked by owls, plus others showing bearded farmers with long toes and wings teasing grain up from the soil, lists of animals slaughtered for annual celebrations, and which cities had contributed what to the temples.

    No way to know where they've gone, what they were. The inventory sheets were burned, too.

    All this precious ephemera stored in holes under rugs, or passed to border guards high in the mountains at night.

    Or a clay tablet dropped in the rush, rolled over by tanks, now just regular dust.

                                              – Nina

The Unmaking of Evidence

So brilliant a thief was Sargon, the Sumerian Father of Imperialism, that he perfected the art of stealing something from someone and making them think they were getting a gift.

He let the subjects of his newly acquired city-states keep their local deities and rituals, but he had his spiritual leaders imbue the deities with new qualities that would elevate Sargon's culture.

He perfected a technique for making seized people feel like they had not been seized but more like the two cultures had been merged in a sort of marriage. Any coercion was forgotten for the greater good.

Over 4,000 years ago Sargon – the public relations mastermind with the outer space name – invented the cultural attack known now as "co-optation," making use of writers, artisans and scholars as much as soldiers.

Hymns were repeated until the language began to feel natural. Like there had never been another way of speaking or thinking. He let the subject choose a favorite of the two hymns his daughter the Priestess had written, and that would become their official hymn. They picked the one they felt best represented their culture. They felt empowered by freedom of choice.

Co-optation, or the re-signification of previously threatening beliefs is still a popular ruling class tactic today.

For this technique to work, it's important that the new truths "make sense" within the old frames of reference, but it's more important that the captured not be given any room to question the new ideas dressed up in familiar old clothes.

The ideas must be simple and consistent. If the conquered begin to question the ideas, they may revolt, then the militia must be brought back again, which is expensive and dangerous. Although unlikely, especially if the workers are well-entertained, there's always the possibility of a successful rebellion.

In an early book, *SynopEthics*, Enron Scabbard called Sargon, "The most effective Jargon-Juggler the world had ever known."

How [Gil] Learned About Nature

It is middle-of-nowhere Virginia, 1976, the Bicentennial. Fan-shaped flags hang from white balconies. A father tells his daughter that lying has made her ill. Lying will make her sicker. She knows this is true.

The three levels of Untruth are branded on her Front-mind. It's the third and highest level he's referring to: the Untruth of Unmanageability. If she worked harder, if she really cared, she could have prevented this illness. Therefore, she wanted the illness, and that fell into the second category of lie: Bad Faith. Pretending to want one thing when one really wants another. Pretending to want to be an effective, productive member of a family and church community, when really one prefers to resist contribution, one prefers to Other themselves from the whole so they make themselves ill. They want to dwell in Mental Rot Stew but will not express that desire directly.

He takes her to the clinic, drops her off. The chairs are shiny like jewelry, plastic beads, shaped like spoons. The nurse, with a serious expression asks the 12-year-old how she got pregnant. Jennifer says, she guesses from lying.

Do you have a boyfriend?

Yes. But she wasn't allowed to see him except at school. He wasn't a Synopologist. He was her first friend who was not in the Church. Skinny with red hair, he was good at wood shop and nice to her.

(She'd been going to the public school where the enemy children went ever since she was eight years old when the police had come to the house. There'd been a crackdown on all the cult kids on the compound, and the parents were forced to send them to the local public school, not wanting to go through the hassle of making a school on the compound for only a handful of kids. Most of the Synopologists there were single or recently divorced. The boy had been her friend.)

And have you done things together?

"What kind of things?"

Specificity-Lack. Loosey-Goosey. The nurse was manufacturing a Near-Untruth with Tonal Deviance and Omissionary Fishing.

The first category of lie was the necessary kind, not manufactured for one's Self but, when endangered by a Syn-Oppressive as legibility management, a Salvo should be first attempted.

Jennifer employed Salvo. She tilted her eyes downward, slightly right, as if shielding retrospect, offering for Interpretation guilt or submission. Which was, of course, the same thing.

Have you and your boyfriend engaged in sexual intercourse, Jennifer?

No. Not with him. She felt protective of him.

Her father had used that technique to discipline her for Syn-Oppressive behavior. It was a severe kind of training, condoned if not prescribed in Enron Scabbard's manual on Re-configuring Syn-Oppressive children.

"I have experimented with boys," she told the nurse. "I have been told that is normal for a girl my age." She became very skilled at Affect Management. That was her main talent. "But never with my friend."

Who then? A cousin? Somebody who visits your daddy?

Jennifer experienced the warm signal of Syn-Oppressive Bad Faith. All the pressure rose up to her head and throat like the waving air over a boiling pot. The urge to Silence her False Self grew wispy.

She heard a voice like hers come from her own mouth. It truly seemed like she hadn't made the decision to say it: "My brothers. My father." *Once on the boat, Enron Scabbard.* She didn't say that. She could never say that. Many times the Said can be Unsaid, but sometimes it can't. Once it makes a Causal Object with Material Effects, it can't be Unsaid easily.

At once, Jennifer understood two things. That she was curious what might happen, and that she already knew. She was in a Self-Selected Doubt Trance. It was one of her main problems.

The nurse slowly and carefully explained the difference between getting pregnant and getting punished. The nurse was kind. A very skilled presenter of False Empathy. She would contact the authorities. They would come and ask Jennifer questions. If she slipped with them like she had with the nurse, the Church wouldn't even bother to excommunicate her; they'd Terminate.

Jennifer was terrified of the authorities. They had come around from time to time and called the Synopologists names – devil worshippers and that kind of thing. A couple of times they had come at night, sniffed around, aiming their flashlights under houses, down outhouse holes, up in the trees, looking for something to bust them on. The community hid no drugs, no stolen goods, and no more firearms than was legal.

"Somebody might just get it in them to burn your whole place down while you're sleeping," a cop had told her in her kitchen not long ago. He was grinning at her, sipping the coffee she'd made for him while the other cops searched.

"Syn-Oppressives are against us at every turn," Jennifer's father reminded his group after the attempted raid. "We have a responsibility to deal with these dangerous enemies as anyone would deal with a harmful pest. All Defensive Tactics against Syn-Oppressives are suitable and legal within the eyes of the Church."

Now everyone on the compound kept their guns loaded. They recited the Ten Syn-Corrects in the main hall five times a day for an entire month. And still had to get their regular workload done.

While she was supposed to be recovering from the abortion, Jennifer left the clinic through the side door marked "Urgent." It was propped open with a wastepaper basket. Nurses in white dresses and white shoes smoked in the alley. They barely glanced at the girl. Girls got in trouble, that was a fact. Nothing to do but let them sort it out as best they could.

Jennifer breathed slowly, focusing on the Ten Syn-Corrects. She made herself Calm to attract less attention as she headed toward the highway through the trees.

Why the Bad Vibes?[1]

"Synopology is without a doubt the most manipulative and dangerous religious multinational corporation in the world today," says former high-ranking member "Tom." In October 1988, as I was beginning to conduct research for this book, Tom contacted me by letter. In fourteen pages he detailed his significant experience and rise to leadership within the group, his evolving disillusionment, and his terrifying escape.

Tom now uses an assumed name and writes from an undisclosed location outside of the United States. He is estranged from his wife and three children, who remain loyal to the group. Although Tom lives in tropical seclusion in fear of being discovered, he describes his life now as "way less twisted than that bad trip I was on in Virginia."

Tom sent the following classified information about the origins of "human suffering" in the Synopology belief system, which is unavailable to all but the most highly-ranked Synopology officials. This story has since been corroborated by several former qualifying members of Synopology who each demanded that I respect their anonymity.

The following story* reveals the religion's myth of the origin of all contemporary human woes, and the need for Synopology's special brand of techno-spiritual intervention. Hold on to your beer-can hat, because this origin myth is a rollicking ride:

* From *Alien Origins: The Postwar Mytho-Logic of America's Home-Grown Religions*, pp. 46-49. (1976)
Reprinted by permission of author, Dr. Juliana Von Trout

Seventy-five million years ago, there was an alien patriarch named Syn-0. Syn-0 was in charge of thirteen planets including Earth. All his planets were dying due to overpopulation, because the planets' inhabitants could not control themselves. The planets could no longer support everyone, which caused the people to develop a mass viral brain disorder called "Scarcity Thinking."

Scarcity Thinking eventually led the inhabitants to begin impulsively destroying themselves, each other, and their habitats.

Syn-0 could not cure the disease of Scarcity Thinking, and his best propaganda campaigns were unsuccessful in convincing citizens that reproduction was an unnecessary, dangerous, and avoidable by-product of some types of sex.

Despite his great power, Syn-0 suddenly felt like a little boy inside. But this sense of powerlessness was only in his head, because in truth he had unimaginable authority and resources.

He soon devised a plan for a complete, foolproof solution.

Nearly all citizens of his thirteen planets in four solar systems, which Syn-0 called "Dumbfucks," would be destroyed and, along with them, the Scarcity Thinking Virus.

Syn-0 understood he needed to start over. He would allow a handful of his friends and lovers (who showed no signs of the Virus) to survive if they would help eradicate the Dumbfucks and the Scarcity Thinking Virus. He called his army "Syn-0's Scarcity-Free Survivors." (SSFSs)

Syn-0 determined that he could get all of his citizens in one place by threatening them with imprisonment for Intergalactic Tax Fraud. He sent out official-looking letters inviting all the Dumbfucks to his planet for income tax audits.

When the aliens from the thirteen defeated planets arrived at Syn-O's IRS headquarters, they were given injections of Cocaine, Dilaudid and Thorazine to paralyze them and cause them to feel elated, rather than frightened. Unable to defend themselves or flee, the interplanetary dupes were wheeled into futuristic-looking space planes.

The SSFSs flew the pleasantly buzzing captives to special outer space "forests" on several unmarked planets where highly sensitive interrogations normally were held. Once there, the hundreds of billions of paralyzed Dumbfucks were rolled in wheelchairs to the edges of the planets' hydro-electrical generators.

Syn-O then pushed a round, red, flashing button with his long, alien finger and blew up all of the electricity generators at once, causing all dams to burst. Electricity went crazy on the water and everyone exploded.

So, the first phase of Syn-O's plan was stunningly successful. Everyone died except Syno and the SSFSs.

"The Disempowering Would Happen At The Level Of Consciousness..."

For the time being, there was no more reason to worry about things getting out of control anymore because of Overpopulation and The Virus (plus resource mismanagement, species disavowal, simultaneous and contradictory truths, slippery signification, urgent and relentless yearning, nagging sense of dissatisfaction, confusion, and fear of pointlessness, painful transformations, and garden-variety free-floating despair).

But Syn-O soon discovered that only the Dumbfucks' bodies had died! Their acorporeal spirits (known as Zzzatans), remained threateningly alive.

The blast had put the Zzzatans in a deep sleep, but soon they would wake up, and these zillions of angry Zzzatans would seek justice. And revenge.

Syn-O needed to come up with a fast plan for what to do with all the Zzzatans, or else there'd soon be hordes of them screaming through outer space.

More terrifying than that, the disembodied-yet-sentient and animate souls would, in a short time and under the right conditions, become people again. (The unique capacity to develop from formlessness to form and back to formlessness again, is in Synopology the standard definition of "living." (See Chapter 11 of *What Is Synopology?* (1961), "Is the Sign Alive?" for so-called semiotic health applications.) If the Zzzatans were allowed to develop bodies again, those bodies would reproduce.

Syn-O and his trusted advisors had hit a wall. They could imagine no way to eliminate all the Zzzatans entirely. But Syn-O's youngest and brightest SSFS had a shrewd idea.

"It's War, And It's Been This Same War For 75 Million Years."

Jennifer, the young strategist, dreamed up the solution Syn-O had been looking for all along: To disorient the souls so thoroughly that even when they re-acquired bodies they would be harmless! The disempowering would happen at the level of consciousness, so the Dumbfucks would become entirely trustworthy in states of either form or formlessness!

Syn-O captured all the stray Zzzatans by allowing them to jump by the thousands into the bodies of his most loyal SSFSs. Then he took the former resource-guzzling Dumbfucks, now stuffed into the bodies of his lesser friends, to a giant movie theater right down the road from where he lived.

Syn-O used his newest weapon of mass entertainment to implant the poor Zzzatans with confounding beliefs. By showing them special 3-D propaganda films about the history of humanity, Syn-O would convince all the Zzzatans to latch onto a whole bunch of ideas that would seem completely "true" and would simultaneously freak them out at the deepest levels of the spirit.

These natural-seeming narratives would deprive the Zzzatans of their sense of collective and personal power, and the Zzzatans would try to overcompensate forever, always sensing they

"They left the movies and paced around, stunned, not knowing what to do with themselves."

were somehow failing.

The films presented entertaining stories titled, "God vs. The Devil," "Why Masculinity is An Energy," and "Gestalt Therapy: Play-Acting Your Way To Mental Ruin."

Afterward the bewildered over-entertained Zzzatans left the movies and paced around, stunned, not knowing what to do with themselves, because their whole history was new to them.

They'd become educated.

Thus civilized, they were in no position to fly back to their ruined homes. There was nowhere for them to go, because every place was the same: dangerous and uncertain.

As a defense against this newly mystifying universe, the Zzzatans inhabiting the bodies of Syn-O's most loyal troops gathered together in freaked out disempowered communities and began to act out.

So, just as the movies had predicted – because the Oedipal Dynamic is an irreversible narrative law – Syn-O was soon overthrown by his own loyal army of SSFSs, which was teeming with misguided Zzzatans.

They imprisoned Syn-0 rather than killing him because, once he died, he'd become a Zzzatan too, and then they'd have to welcome him into their cause.

The rebels locked Syn-0 in a mountain on one of his former secret interrogation planets. There is no way he can escape.

At this moment, he is alive and as potentially dangerous as ever. And the Zzzatans are alive, too, having reproduced for 75 million years, transmitting themselves from one generation to the next through "genes."

Every human on Earth is thickly populated by dazed, hypersensitive, violent Zzzatans. These vengeful, former Dumbfucks cause all unruly human problems that result from deeply ingrained beliefs that are based in pure fiction, created to confound them.

Like invisible neuronal gremlins, Zzzatans tickle forth insomnia, accident and indecency. They spawn forgetting, gripping, grappling, failure, reluctance, deceit, and desire.

They beget AIDS, addiction, global warming, political torture, mental illness, starvation, rape, suicide, domestic violence, and imperialism. In fact, you name it, if it's bad, it comes from the Zzzatans.

Our world continues to pay the price for Syn-0's mass-murder and brainwashing.

Only by using the patented Synopology Method can human beings locate and dislodge their own Zzzatans. It is up to each of us to help bring the universe back to a state of "No-Syn," through diligent practice of Synopology.

As Enron Scabbard has said, "If you are not part of the solution, you are part of the problem."

If you refuse to support the Church of Synopology, you will be considered an Enemy of the Church, and the Church, using an approach it calls simply "You Lose," may be forced to destroy you for the benefit of future generations.

For Synopologists, it's a serious war, and it's been this same war for 75 million years.

Which side are you on?

"If you are not part of the solution, you are part of the problem."
– Enron Scabbard

*Warning: Synopologists Believe That Reading This Story Before Reaching Secret Decoder Level III ($300,000 and up), Will Cause One To Become "Sick-Made" With "Pneumonia" Or Another "Disease," Or even to Harm One's "Self," Without Apparent Cause.

August 21, 2006

Earth calling Winky, come in Winky:

[Gil] always identified with the male heroes in books and movies. But she identified with every other kind of character too, every setting, and every narrative architecture.

If freedom of will is contingent upon coherence of self and desire, and [Gil] was therefore not coherent, then she obviously had no free will. So, no one can blame her for the things she did. Not even the things she did to me.

Her mind made her believe she was a City, then a man, then a child. Back and forth. None of these ways of being conscious remembered any other way. They were distinct. That's how [Gil] was different from those of us who hold two or more incompatible desires or beliefs at the same time. The word for that, I've just learned, is "akrasia."

Regular people find all sorts of amazing ways to deal with akrasia. For example, the conundrum, "I want to live / I want to die" might resolve in thrill-seeking or punk rock behavior, which is a way to fulfill both desires without acknowledging either. A common form of akrasia happens when we read. We know the character does not exist as a person, but we also get ourselves to believe they do exist so we can engage emotionally with the character. This is a way of creating a false sense of connection. I was actually reading something about that in St. Augustine's Confessions, of all places, a couple of nights ago. He said,

> When [a person] suffers in his own person, it usually is called misery: when he compassionates others, then it is mercy. But what sort of compassion is this for feigned and theatrical passions? For the auditor is not called on to aid others, but only to grieve: and he applauds the actor of these fictions the more, the more he grieves. And if the calamities of those persons (whether of old times or mere fiction) be so acted, that the spectator is not moved to tears, he goes away disgusted and criticizing; but if he be moved to grief, he stays intent and weeps for joy.

Emotional engagement with narrative is not really akratic because the reader is aware of the contradiction real/not real, and she engages with full consent. She adopts a symbolic, aesthetic stance in order to experience an effect. So it's different from total incoherence of selfhood. Or anyway, that's what the experts say.

People with Multiple Personality Disorder, as it was called then, or Dissociative Identity Disorder, as it's called now, sometimes use a little object to help them hold it together. It can be a rubber ball or a stone or a tiny stuffed fox on a key chain. Because a person's identity is contingent upon context, the object becomes the perpetual context. The transitional object can be a person, but it's better to use something else. A person is too unpredictable to be a reliable context. Because people lie and change their minds.

But you already know that.

Nanu Nanu, Nina

Anna Joy Springer

Worst Thing!

Eye tight
on the score, full stop.
Unengaged, but alive.
Superfree.

It's fiction. Deceit.
Crafting the seductive
safe hold, strong grip.

Here's your mass appeal:
Yearning, striving.
Interpreting keenly,
wild, swinging.

For an ending place.
A little red
burrow
that stays.

How To Fill In the Blank

Gilgamesh went to the temple to give the Goddess his answer to her proposal. Inanna opened the door for him. Her hair was white, and the skin of her neck was loose. Her eyes were sad and lined and clear. She wore an undyed linen dress. She looked nothing like a Queen.

Inanna led him through the temple to her private quarters, then through the doorway to her garden. He followed her. For courage, he conjured an image of Enkidu.

Inanna sat Gilgamesh down in the small cedar grove in the garden of her temple. She did not touch his curling hair. She thanked him for the lumber, for the monster Humbaba's head. She thanked him for his prowess and devotion. She did not touch his strong chest.

She said, "I will not force you to marry me if you can answer my question: There is one thing humans may know that gods may only imagine," she said to the King. "What is it?"

Gilgamesh answered, "Death."

She said that she knew death. She'd been killed in the underworld. She told him that she'd give him another guess.

He said, "Then, sickness."

She said that she knew sickness; she'd vomited before she died. She told him to try harder, to think.

He said, "Old age, poverty, regret, weakness, fear, none of these things can the gods know."

She told him she had, in fact, known all these things. Moreover, she knew their causes and cures. And he'd used up all of his chances.

"If I marry you," he said, "you will kill me when you are through with me." He listed her past cruelties, which were well-known by all.

"I could kill you right now," said Inanna, "if that were my plan. But that is not my plan, handsome King. My plan is to marry you so that you'll concede your power to me. Isn't that what they tell you in King school? Listen. I will give you one more chance because I'm at an unfair advantage, and you are being so brave right now. I will tell you a story. If at the end of this story you guess the answer to my question, I will let you go free to be with your friend. You will spend the rest of your days in excitement and plundering. You will make a great name for yourself and you will be feared. You will have all the power any man has ever known. You will obtain the secret to immortality. You will become a god, much more powerful than even I. If you lose, it will not be so terrible for you. But if you win, you will have everything you could ever imagine wanting."

What choice did he have, weaponless, tempted, there in her temple, in her grove?

"If you guess the right answer to my question. I will tell you the story of my unstoppable pursuit of power. I will tell you how I won it, and why I'm so willing to give it away."

Consider The Complex Concept "Communicable"

1. That may be communicated or imparted.

1534 LD. Berners Gold Bk. M. Aurel (1546) The goddis haue made all thyges communicable to men mortall, excepte immortalitie. **(1577) tr. Bullinger's Decades (1592)** Properties of God, communicable to no creature.

2. a. Of diseases: Contagious or infectious by contact. See CONTAGION.

1710 STEELE Tatler No. 10 There is a communicable Sickness, which, it is feared, will end in a Pestilence.

1879 MACLAGAN in 19th Cent. 810 When we wish to say that a disease is produced by personal contact with a person suffering from it we call it communicable.

Synopology Test Method: Syn-Correct Assessment
For Children (Ages 3-7)

INSTRUCTIONS:

Place the Electropsychosigndefibber on the child's head and fasten cans over ears. In the child-sized headgear, tomato paste cans work better than beer or soda cans. Make the child look you in the eye while answering the following questions. Do not accept as an excuse for a jump in the meter that the child was "just nervous." Kids are crawling with newly reborn Zzzatans and must have their perceptions cleansed quickly in order to be of immediate help in the battle against global uncertainty, confusion and servitude. Only after they have acknowledged and confessed their mismanagement of signs can they be trusted to engage honestly in Syn-Correct Semiotic Management (SCSM). Repeat the first battery of questions until the child's meter reads "Absent," then proceed to the next phase of applying the Ten Syn-Corrects to each question.

• What has somebody told you not to tell?

• Have you ever decided you didn't know whether you liked some member of your family, housing group, or Synopology?

• Have you ever decided to employ a half-hearted Salvo with the hope of getting to lie outright?

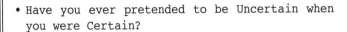

- Have you ever pretended to be Uncertain when you were Certain?

- Have you ever made yourself confused or hurt yourself to make somebody sorry?

- How have you made someone else guilty or Uncertain?

- Have you ever done something you shouldn't when you were supposed to be in bed or asleep?

- Have you ever told others Untruths about someone, especially someone from the Church?

- Have you ever tried to make others believe that your parents or teachers were cruel to you or made you believe Untruths?

- Have you ever offered as an excuse for something you have done wrong or misunderstood that you are only a child?

- Have you ever expressed an Untruth by crying when there was no good reason to cry?

- Have you ever expressed an Untruth by making too much fuss over a little hurt?

- Have you ever told on anyone?

- Will you ever tell on me?

Combatants of the Church will try to smash us in court for this. They'll say children should not be subjected to these mandatory interviews. Any such critic is the Sworn Enemy of the Church and should be subjected to You Lose tactics. They confuse truth with sentiment. Do not be swayed by the Zzzatanick Sign-Distortion called "Innocence."

— Enron Scabbard, 1964

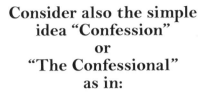

Consider also the simple idea "Confession" or "The Confessional" as in:

Lily-livered,
Enemy,
Solipsistic,

Ill-equipt,
Manipulative,
Unsoldierly,

Girly,
Lesbian,
Childish,

Pulpy,
Cheap,
Cliché,

Tortured,
Melodramatic,
Red,

Embarrassing,
Pained,
and Prone.

An undesired degrading sacrifice.

A seeking of refuge in shame.

THE FOREST OF DESPOTS' DAUGHTERS

After giving her sire a fresh baby girl, the despot's daughter will escape, hiding in the thick forest.

Not knowing others like her live there in the Forest of Despots' Daughters, she will faint when she finds her mothers, sisters and aunties grouped around a fire, twitching and moaning. Their eyes have hearts beating inside. They boil whatever scraggly weed they find, and drink the soup to see what it does. Poison? Miscarriage? Ecstasy? Tasty?

Obviously, from time to time, during a slow period or election season, they will be gathered up and questioned by officials from outside the forest. Here's what the officials will ask:

Have you ever avoided your duty as a daughter?

Have you decided you're too good for us?

Have you found something ugly attractive?

Have you ever confided in outsiders?

Familiar with interrogation tactics, having grown up with the despot, the daughters will lie skillfully. They will play the coquette. They will perform exquisite blowjobs. The officers will leave one way or another.

During questioning many daughters are accidentally drowned. The most influential despots have the officials lock their daughters in dark boxes and flown to an island no one can get to. They will be left there forever, or until the despot retires.

The drowned ones' graves will go unmarked, except for a warning, a thin crescent moon lying dead on its back, stuck in the dirt on a popsicle stick.

The moon is a symbol of where the girls came from before they became despots' daughters. The crazy forest ladies are thought to have flown down from the moon. Which is why they must be questioned, and why some must be drowned. They are dangerous in both their knowledge and lies.

In their indiscretion and passion, the despots' daughters consort with four-legged beasts, not to mention the ones with wings and fins. Truly they'll fuck anything they can, give birth to flopping things with weird patches of hair, flat eyes, one tooth. They must not be allowed to mate, mutants will plunder the Earth.

Of course, mate they have already done. The despots' daughters are their own daughters, too. The forest is peopled by mutants who hit themselves and stink.

They have inbred and become various. Species, texts, viruses curling sneakily through the bloodstream. They are tricky, the witches. They change shape, they fly to and from the moon, to and from the prison on the hidden island, they enjoy anarchy, they are bitter, will not take their meds.

To get rid of them entirely, one official calculates, they will have to feed the old crones thousands of poisons for thousands of years, then pump in gas, then chop the whole forest down. One must burn them to ash, put the ash in a box, send the box out to sea with the garbage. Let it float up on the shore of the hidden island and rot, so the ones imprisoned feel lucky to be warm and alive in their pens.

The despots report that they are unworried by these freakish women who choose to hide away in the forest shaking their cooking sticks, squeaking threats.

The despots say that these blights will burn themselves out of their own accord, before they can do any damage. They are weaponless, pathetic.

They say that the girls, illiterate and unable to record their own lies, are harmless, so let them dance and boil their roots. Let them ride through the nights on the backs of bright smears.

What harm could they do but annoy, like spiders or beggars? It's not like they have something anyone wants anymore, after all.

The despots repeat a prayer each night before bedding down: "Don't look at the moon, it's ugly."

October 28, 2006

Dear Winky,

Unsmiling, defiant, we denied being victims or daughters.

[Gil] will tell you she was one of five kids -- three girls, two boys. She'll tell you all about tangled, tabloid sex relationships, the whole family pairing off, forcing acts, enduring them, or just climbing up into each other's beds at night like puppies. [Gil]'s mother wasn't around. If she ever existed, she'd died or been killed. That's what she told me, anyway. Who knows what she'll tell you.

You already know her father was a murderer. Of not just her mother but of strangers, too. Women came into [Gil]'s house and never left, like roaches on vacation in the Roach Motel. Women too poor for anyone to bother looking for, hookers and junkies. You've seen the grainy TV dramatizations, Virginia women planted in the dirty earth like spells. [Gil]'s father had hidden the victims' corpses, one on top of another there in the soil after conducting his experiments. He was practicing something, [Gil] didn't know what. But wouldn't the cops have checked the cult first? Wouldn't the dogs smell the bodies?

You may not believe her. I didn't at first, but then I did. Because, why not? It could have happened. Cult-rapist-serial-killers must have families all over the place, why wouldn't they?

What kind of daughter does a man who kills women have? [Gil] had a regular look of horror in her eyes, a pretty look that

seemed like poetry to me. But what kind of daughter? Oh, I'm sure, all kinds of daughters. Nice ones, mean ones, scared ones, happy ones, dumb ones, brilliant ones, all kinds of possibility for these little girls.

[Gil] for one, had spent a lot of time chained-up under the bathroom sink for being subordinate. That's the kind of girl she was. But nobody could prove any of that shit happened. It's her word against whoever's.

Looking for clues to solve the mystery is like trying to read a hymn that's 5000 years old, and you've only got these clay shards. Plus the hymn is written in a language nobody's ever seen. The clay has already broken up and worn away from weather or any number of things, whichever bombs are falling, conspiratorial revision, what have you. And now your touch is turning it into powder.

Her stories might as well have been scratched like names into the seashore; they left no artifact. They left only grit in the bed, which irritated [Gil] as if I'd dumped it from my purse. Sandy nothing, like ellipses between verses. A bed full of bracketed empties. A body made of them.

Without evidence, all I had for fact was [Gil]'s body and what it produced. So that is what I studied. Her muscles, the watery blue of her eyes, her kidney-bean torso, fists in balls. And I catalogued the things she said when we closed our eyes and let ourselves go all blank and on fire, pounding, the things I heard myself whisper back to her or yell. Hurtful things. The very cruelest ones I could think of. The insults came so easily.

Truthfully existing side-by-side in the dark air around us was what the words meant and what I really meant if you took out the words. Both ways of meaning became more alive in relation.

After practicing my violence so often, the practice seemed to tilt toward virtuosity.

Like maybe the crime shows dramatizing the psychological evolution of a sexual predator were wrong. Maybe there was a kind who didn't drown neighborhood cats and burn ants as a boy. Maybe he didn't listen to Ozzy in the dark while his single-mother balled some guy in the storeroom of the diner where she worked.

Maybe there was another kind of psycho-killer sex fiend. At some point she discovered she was not the regular small town art girl she thought she was. She had a passion, a talent. She had to follow her calling. Her lover cheered her on, told her to keep going, more. Her love told her, "Hurt me more."

The girl became convinced that she soon might kill her lover. At first the idea scared the shit out of her, and then it began to seem like a reasonable conclusion. Her lover said, "Please, more." The girl believed what she was doing was love. Then she did it again and again until her arrest.

In the documentary everyone said, "I'd never have guessed, she was such a bright girl." You can see the whole thing play out.

I did. I saw that in my heart I could be anyone, even the "father", and that I owned nothing, nothing of me, not a damn thing. The one I thought I was, that one was gone, just a thought not a person.

And I'm a different one now, too.

Say, "Knock knock."

"Knock knock."

"Who's there?"

But that is a spiritual topic. And I was talking about fathers.

Maybe before Synopology, when [Gil]'s father first fell in love with Jenny's mother, it was as surprising for him as my own destructive urgency was for me. It could have been kinky for him, being gentle, like being mean was kinky for me.

But after they married the love left, right? Because that's the way the story always goes. And he went right back to normal. He petted his kids then made them whimper until he filled with pure white bliss, said some weird Synopology bullshit and came. Then he put them to work in the Church and ate his turkey pot pie.

That's what [Gil] told me.

She'll probably have a different story for you. She was the person she was with me, and she'll be different with you.

You could think of Dissociative Identity Disorder as just an extreme form of personality contingency, with some amnesia. It still sounds pretty normal to me.

Love,
Nina

Security For Leaders

[Gil] took it upon herself to help [Blinky] survive in the City. It was what any friend or parent would do. It was time for him to know about predators.

She masked her face with mirrored police sunglasses pulled her sweatshirt hood up over her baseball cap. She wrapped Blinky in a black handkerchief and pinned it to her undershirt, so his ear was barely visible above the collar of her favorite flannel. In this way she could whisper to him without being spotted.

They rode the 22 bus to the Golden Gate Synopology Center. They sat at the park across the street, and [Gil] lit a cigarette. "If they knew I was here they would take me inside, and then we'd have to fight," she said quietly. Blinky shuddered without knowing why.

"I have to keep you safe from them," she said. You'd be the perfect hit because you are frightened and seek reassurance. Here is what they will do. They will offer you a cup of coffee, the coffee will be strong and good. They will point out a plate of cookies. They will suggest you enjoy a free shoulder massage. You will be suspicious, but they will seem warm, and since you are lonely and new in the City, you will give them a chance. They will hand you a brochure with an image of a energy producing dam on the front. They will appeal to your disillusionment. They will massage your ears, your trunk, and tell you how satisfied, how confident they are now. They will tell you there is a better way. And this is how they will try to take you from me. Their offers will seem harmless. They will ask some coded questions to see whether you are a spying enemy of the Church. You will pass their test. They will seduce you with promises of safety and certainty."

Blinky felt sleepy wrapped up against [Gil]'s chest with the cigarette smoke hovering in the sunlight.

[Gil] pointed out a skinny yuppie reaching for a free cookie, grinning like he was winning a game. Like he'd eat some treats, charm some zealots, and drop the pamphlet in the can on the corner.

"See that one, he's swallowed his masculine confidence pill. He believes in the role he presents. He thinks he's safe. But he will follow that pretty one, see her, that one, he will follow her inside. The pretty girls are trained to flirt when they're fishing for converts. I never had to fish, they started that after I left. When she gets him into the interview office, she will tell him things about the nature of his experience, things he's never told anyone before. He feels seen for the first time. She offers him a solution to his confusion. She gives him another cookie. It's easy. She walks him to that ATM machine on the corner. Lots of the women who don't want to sign up still withdraw the cost of the first class. They're polite or embarrassed to say no. Or they're intimidated. Then they go to the first class because they've already paid for it. And the first class is what we called, "Hard Sell." It's brilliant. You'd be surprised by how many people have never told their secrets to a stranger. You'd be surprised by how easy it is to make a person vulnerable by listening."

Blinky nodded his head to let her know he was with her.

"So, after a few courses, that yuppie that just got fished will believe the Church makes him stronger in his communication with others. He will seem more self-possessed. He will successfully negotiate a raise at work and will tell his girlfriend to give him some space. He will learn that the more he gives himself entirely to the process, the more freedom and clarity he will have. He will feel his new friends understand him and care. He will enjoy the new sense of community. He will feel safe."

Blinky's eyelids grew heavy. [Gil]'s heartbeat comforted him. He liked the way she smelled, and her T-shirt was soft.

"But there's nothing wrong with feeling safe," you might say. You might say you felt safe in your forest before you came here. The joke is, in order to feel safe, you have to define a threat. More importantly for your sense of ongoing recognizable safety, you have to maintain it. Slight attacks are energizing and reassuring."

When the Church started getting attacked on a larger scale, back when she was still in it, the congregation became more unified. But then the attackers won a court case demanding the children be sent to school and taken to hospitals when they were sick or hurt.

So Enron Scabbard began to focus entirely on security. [Gil]'s father became Director of Defense. He hid himself away in his den to strategize against the Church's opponents. He let the children tend to themselves. Meanwhile Scabbard wrote new edicts, sometimes three or four a week, and sent them to Synopology Centers around the world. Each one began, "Now is a time of War."

Scabbard was paranoid, true, but in this case he was rightfully concerned. In the 1980s the Church was hunted by powerful players. The IRS was after him. And the Feds were watching the Church, especially the kids' facilities. So were the media, the American Medical Association, the Council of Churches, and Cultwatch. More and more enemies gathered. His edicts restricted members' access to misinformation. They were safe as long as they banded together.

Enron's fear was the children. They were less predictable, had different fears. There were laws to protect children, and the warrants for raids on compounds were always granted on suspicion of child abuse. This tactic of going after the children was the universal strategy to dismantle spiritual organizations competing financially with the patronizing monotheistic babysitter religions. The enemies would always create a Misinformation Flow in order to convince the public that alternative religions sacrificed children.

And children were dangerous. Because of the Learned Symbolic Law of Oedipal Retaliation. Even the loyal ones would eventually try to overthrow him.

Scabbard instituted abortions for every pregnancy, including a mandatory class on procreation as Bad Faith. For the members coming in with children, he demanded that the kids be released to a well-endowed child-rearing facility, where the young could be educated in a wholesome environment outside the City and prevented from interfering with their parents' spiritual development.

"So, Blinky, since I'm your guardian here in the City, I'd be considered your parent. If I were still a Synopologist, I'd have to think of you as a potential enemy of the Church, until you proved you were weren't. You'd have to sign a legal contract stating you would work for the Church for ten-thousand lifetimes, and that you were signing the document of your own free will as an adult. If, when you were 18, you had still refused to sign the contract, you would be subjected to worse and worse punishments and coercion, psychological torture, illness, menacing, all that, until you were able to escape or you caved. I signed one, and that's why they're after me now.

"But the real reason the Church fears kids is because they pull at their parents' heart-strings and undermine the training. It takes many courses before most parents learn to release their belief in 'my children.' That's why they got rid of my mother.

"Did I tell you they killed my mother?

"Now they don't even give parents the chance to be swayed by sentimentality and attachment. The only unsecurable intelligence is love, which is, as every true Synopologist knows, one of the top three worst Over-Saturated Empty Signifiers."

But Blinky didn't hear why the Church was afraid of the intertwined constructs, "Child" and "Love." Blinky had fallen asleep.

[Gil] was worried her friend might be sick, he slept so much. She'd told him classified secrets that supposedly no one below a certain level in the Church could know without their Zzzatans retaliating by causing a sickness the listener was not yet skilled enough to fight with his will.

Winner of the Big Victim Contest

It got so I would see a man holding a little girl, his hand supporting her back, his hand the width of her back, and I would see a predator. "Is touching her turning him on?" I'd think, "Are his arms the strongest, most terrible cage? How long's it gonna be? How many minutes or hours before he sneaks her away somewhere private?"

Was it crazy to worry that father meant danger? Was it prurience? My superhero delusion delight? An oversimplified answer to all the world's woes?

Freud thought childhood sexual abuse accounted for neurosis before his colleagues shot him down. Surely molestation wasn't so prevalent as the high numbers of neurotic women would indicate. Surely not.

I had never thought much one way or another about fathers before I moved to San Francisco. But then I learned the big secret. Almost every girl I met had been molested, gang-raped, fiddled, or hounded by one family guy or the other. Not just dykes, but every kind of woman.

Everyone had a copy of *The Courage to Heal* on their bookshelves alongside *Our Bodies, Ourselves, Bastard Out of Carolina, Hothead Paisan, The Cancer Journals, The Cunt Coloring Book*, and the *Encyclopedia of Natural Remedies*. All of them were "survivors" not "victims."

It was time for us to stop thinking of ourselves as victims, or else we'd always be victimized. We had to "break the silence." And it's true, we did have to.

My mother wasn't buying it. She said it seemed like I *wished* I'd been molested, I talked about it so much.

In my mother's mind, my lust was for a sort of empty capital, like the right kind of roller skates or Jordache, only more annoying for her to hear about.

Maybe all us San Francisco girls were imagining things. Maybe her husband didn't cop a feel here and there, watch me dress, lay on the couch with his porn and his dick in his hand. Maybe I was having someone else's memory. I wanted to be in with the in-crowd. I wanted to win the prize.

Maybe I did. Maybe all of us did, and maybe most fathers are like in the movies: Rolling Easter eggs on the White House lawn and tousling our hair.

Maybe we all wanted attention and lied to get hugs, to make friends. Maybe it'd teach us a lesson if all the regular people in regular people land just pretended we didn't exist at all. Maybe we still want too much attention and telling our bad daddy secrets is not the way to get it now or ever. Maybe we can't have the big prize. Maybe the prize is irrelevant.

What's a father for, again? A strong hand, the mortgage, kicking the tire? Grilling the meat, lifting the box, throwing the pigskin on Thanksgiving day? Who fucking knows.

Where I came from, there were no fathers. Us latchkey kids with single moms working carcinogenic affirmative action jobs in work boots watched TV for our father myths. We compiled Cleavers and Huxtables and Simpsons in our mental storyboards and put them in the "Over There" category. Over There in Nowhere Land. We compiled dictators and psycho-killers and televangelists. Cheaters, Beaters, Breadwinners, Kings, Princes, Salesmen, Cops, and Thieves. Soldiers. Heroes and Anti-heroes. Man versus nature, Man versus God, Man versus man versus man versus man.

They all bored us to death with their pat little make-believe answers and outbursts. Their hair-trigger low grade terror, how it made them dangerous or how it made them easy. We learned to freeze, please, and appease.

Now we were unlearning just as hard as we could.

November 12, 2006

Dear Winky,

It totally makes sense that you'd ask me about my own father. You're a quick study, you know the right questions to ask, you'll do fine.

There's not much to it, really. My father died seven months before [Gil] did. My mother drove up to San Francisco to tell me in person, which was unlike her. We went out for sushi in the Mission before she went home, and it was like this heavy tight nothing had happened forever.

Like [Gil], my father died alone in his apartment with lots of rings on his night stand. He spent his government check on trinkets he bought from the crackheads' blankets lined up along the sidewalk next to the docks in San Pedro. He lived on delivered pizzas and cigarettes, three packs a day. He was schizophrenic

and religious, that's all I know. He'd lived on the streets for a long time, but he got an apartment a couple years before he died. So he wasn't one of those dead guys on skid row that nobody knows is dead for 2 days. When I cleaned up his place in San Pedro, I found a picture of him. The picture showed him fat, in coveralls, sitting at a Thanksgiving table holding up the gravy boat. He had a giant beard, but he didn't look crazy. Not dangerous. For no reason I could understand, I completely lost it when I dumped his ashes into the bay. It was like hurling out in sound the noise of an animal in a trap. I wasn't trying to make it happen or to stop it, it just came. It was windy on the boat, so my father's ashes blew back into my face, my mouth. I howled with his ashes on my tongue.

I wanted to know my father, but he died before I could find him. Truthfully I didn't try that hard, I thought I had time. To become more grown up so I'd know what to do. His family, my family, I guess, wouldn't tell me where he lived. They said his sickness would upset me. He cried for no reason when he listened to Rachmaninoff.

I told my grandmother, "I'm not freaked out by crazy people. I have lots of crazy friends, and they're okay." But she still wouldn't tell me where he lived. As far as I knew he was still on the streets somewhere in downtown L.A. with bits of sardine in his beard and piss in his socks.

His family wasn't protecting me from him, no matter what they said. They worried that seeing me grown up would turn up his inner devil parade and they'd take the fallout. I'd get to leave, feeling dutiful or connected or whatever, and they'd have to tend to his meltdown. It's what had happened last time he'd seen me when I was ten. It'd only be worse this time, the way I looked now, the green hair and ripped clothes. Maybe my intentions were selfish. I don't know. I'd just wanted to go to him, to tell him, "Hello. I see you. I'm not afraid." That would have been enough for me. I hope that answers your questions. Sorry for taking so long.

Love,
Nina

THE FOREST OF MOLESTATION CLICHÉS

It's an unforgivable literary sin, the hurt girl cliché.

The critics call it MELODRAMA, spit the word out all half-chewed and globby, into their napkins or onto the floor. Maybe they've been eating free-range organic *New Yorkers* their whole lives and need to keep that light tight taste in their throats forever. Not too tart, not too fatty.

Save the fake yellow cheese for the poor.

Or maybe they just prefer stories of men doing things that men do, getting drunk and climbing buildings, the first time punching another man, or driving around in their cars so alone, leaving the woman they loved because she cheated on them with their so-called best friend. Walking the train tracks for miles. Leaving it all behind. Pulling another swig from the bottle, passing it, saying "fuck yeah," on the rooftop with friends.

Or the inanity, the pressure from all sides, there's no way out and you just keep going. Whoa, it's crazy, you're trapped, there's a nurse with great tits. Problem solved! Just get through the noise, just tune it all out, describe it, tell on it. They laugh so hard they fall out of their trees. They meet each other on the ground, rubbing their bottoms and howl with laughter. How pointless it is, they say, but so funny really, so fucking absurd. It's these small quiet moments that make for great story.

That's what life is, these small alone times.

Keep things believable, the critics remind us again and again.

Jesus Christ, if you HAVE TO have fifty girls slinging gash at the sex-clubs, making some money but still disgusted with their own bodies, AT LEAST make sure no more than ONE of them, ONLY ONE, has a creepy stepfather in her past. Give her a wicked stepmother instead. It's just not believable after a point. God FORBID one's got a case of RITUAL abuse, DEMAND YOUR MONEY BACK if more than one of them does. That's just taking things way too far.

DEMAND YOUR MONEY BACK ANYWAY.

Take the whole cash register, write a letter to the editor.

Teach them to make their stories more ACCESSIBLE, less attacking. No reader likes to feel accused. What matters is heroes and sidekicks. Tell them to make us laugh.

Teach them a lesson, they need a lesson, ignore them, ignore them, and they'll go away. Ignore them, ignore them and call them cliché.

It's like a fucking bad joke, the judges say to each other again. And listen, nobody's laughing.

The phone is ringing.

December 10, 2003

Winky,

It's easy to explain the power games. But how am I supposed to explain leaving someone who's sick and sad when I promised I wouldn't?

I know it seems like a big narcissistic boo hoo for me. 'Oh, I want to perform this self-forgiveness bit, with you and everyone else forgiving me, too.'

Forgiving me for what, which part? The broken promise? Using [Gil] to become more worldly? Believing her fate had been sealed, that she was doomed, giving in to the telos of the cursed? What does that make me, then, if she's the cursed one?

She lost, I won.

It's not what I thought I wanted.

Nina

tautology-

needless repetition of an idea
~~who~~ especially in the words.
other than those of their
immedeate context without
imparting additional
force or clearness

OR -LOGIC- a law that
can be shown on the basis
of certain rules to exclude
no ~~extra rules to exclude~~
logical possibilities.

~~DARWINISM~~
"SURVIVORS
SURVIVe"

Tautology:
"Survivors survive."

Anna Joy Springer

The Tongue, An Eye

Because, in the beautiful fruitful glistening sweet-smelling cheery forest, speckled blue leopards carry golden geese on their heads while they frolic. Eating is fun, dying is fun, communication is fun, negotiations over land and resources are fun, identity politics is fun, seeing is fun, a full spectrum carnival toy. The sun is very round. Its yellow spikes are so far away they seem like pretty jokes, nice and toasty. This is the belief.

(And all the people say: Give me some of that tasty stuff. That party-shocky-rocky stuff. Get me some, get me some, get me some zippy-zang. Zap my worries away, POW! Zap my worries away.)

My girlfriend was ugly but extremely smart. She had a way with words, so her tongue grew long and slick. I think she made me come about a thousand times that year just kissing me.

With her tongue, she also convinced me I was about an inch away from being one of the parasites of the world who feed on trauma, reformers with backpacks and chalk. She convinced me of this as a strategy to get me to prove I wasn't one of the parasites by staying with her all day and tending to her bleeding cervix after I hurt her in bed. That's how good she was. Had I known her cervix was wounded from AIDS and not me, I would have stayed anyway, but she needed things on her terms.

She always kept Blinky there in her room, and he watched me like a tiny bloodshot gargoyle. The dry red bauble didn't want to go back to the forest because he learned that mythical creatures have no real volition. Little asshole. My girlfriend taught the creature to reason, taught it the word "amnesiac".

Forests being fake but true, truth is bitter-sweet.

The caricature found its long nose, which was the source of its particular free will. It held its nose up between its eyes and became cross-eyed for the rest of its life, staring. Eyes stuck that way, the animal finally became endearing to me, like some dumb inbred kitten. My girlfriend kept her crazy-eyed pet in her medicine cabinet as a guard.

I was forbidden to open the door to the cabinet. Cute little wine-colored, crinkly Blinky would rat me out if I went snooping when my girlfriend left the room.

If I would have looked in the cabinet, I would have found her knives, her needles, and AZT. I might have figured out her diagnosis. I might have devoted myself to it. I needed a wound to heal. I needed a stage for my role. I had no idea what living was for if not that.

The Queen of The Dead

Ereshkigal is said to have hated her sister Inanna. Maybe she did and maybe she didn't. All I know is, Inanna wanted to die, and Ereshkigal helped her do it.

When Inanna showed up at the gates of the underworld, Ereshkigal considered her options. The story says:

> She slapped her thigh and bit her lip
> she took the matter into her heart and
> dwelt on it.

Kill Inanna?

"It might be," Ereshkigal thought, "the best thing I could do."

To extinguish the unpredictable and powerful force behind Love and War. Ereshkigal, the Goddess of the Underworld, had a strong sense of social justice but was an extremist like all the gods, nearly ascetic. Passion caused more hurt than everything but poverty. A world without cacoethes would be a peaceful world.

Inanna had come on her own, no one made her. If she choose this nest to make, let her brood in it, pulsing naked as a nerve. She said to her greeter, "Lock the seven doors of the underworld. Open them one by one just wide enough for my sister to slip through. Take away all her fetishes, layer by layer, so she means nothing by the time we meet." Crossing each threshold, Inanna would become human, then human corpse, then spirit, something like nothing.

So, this is the order of seduction into oblivion, and I can understand how that's the thing to court, or at least something to hang around waiting for. I mean, I do it or I hope to do it. I mean, I hope I'm always ready for it.

There Was No Evil Ruler

The world was a shithole of lies, and the only reason everyone didn't kill themselves immediately was because they were too afraid, because they were programmed to believe in the value of human life, because they couldn't face the truth that life was pointless, love was selfish, people were harmful, and sanity was a bullshit concept made up to make people better workers.

All men would become brutal. All women would protect the men, thinking this appeasing behavior would do them some good.

Nothing could help any of us.

There was no evil ruler.

Try harder. Find it. Pick it up. Answer it.

"Make an effort
to remember.
Or, failing that,
invent."

– Monique Wittig

THE FOREST OF
PERIL THAT'S REAL

THE FOREST OF PERIL THAT'S REAL

The concept of a virus as an organism challenges the way we define "life".

Viruses do not respire.

Nor do they display irritability.

They do not move across country, nor do they grow vegetables, nor do viruses write verses plain or weird.

Viruses swim in a gray area where debates about what is alive still rage.

However, viruses do most certainly reproduce, and may adapt to new hosts. Their host, a body, is their world. And their world is dying, and they don't know why.

So, looking from the "bottom up," from the simplest forms displaying the most essential attributes of a living thing, the only real criterion for life may be the ability to replicate, and that systems that contain nucleic acids (except for non-organic replicating objects) are capable of this phenomenon of replicating.

This is the updated definition of desire.

An organism is the unit element of a continuous lineage with an individual evolutionary history which may also experience longing and loss. Therefore, we conclude that the Human Immunodeficiency Viruses are alive. They are beings, they struggle, have values and friends.

Something is poisoning the air and food supply, and the HIVs are afraid. They hide.

This fearful way of living puts the creatures inhabiting a dying world with diminishing resources on edge. They're prone to taking more than they need because it'll be gone tomorrow. They reproduce like crazy. The offspring may help save the world.

A group of their young scurry under stones not knowing why. And it's safe for awhile, but too cold. The air burns out there, where the peril is real. Something hungry, cruel is waiting out there, and everyone knows it. The oxygen fries, and the creatures are gasping, clawing. The world is sputtering out.

A living world holds a dying one's hand at the shitty county hospital.

What is a virus? A set of instructions that are so cold and so desire warmth, they would torch their own homes and kill themselves.

It is encoded, "It's time for a cleaning of house, and God is a ruthless neatfreak."

Most creatures will die gruesome deaths at the hands of their very own worlds. Most worlds will die painful deaths at the hands of their very own creatures.

It is encoded: "Only those who hide best will remain."

Meanwhile, Enkidu

While Ishtar had Gilgamesh in her cedar grove, Enkidu was alone for the first time since he'd left the forest, and homesickness overwhelmed him.

He longed for his forest.

Enkidu set out on foot to taste the water and smell the air that had made him.

But he could not find his forest. It was not where he remembered it being. He wandered and searched, but it was not there.

He had no home to return to.

And yet, this was it.

He made his way back to Uruk with heavy hands and an indescribable ache in his chest.

Pneumonic Devices

Blinky, a pre-literate transitional object, had a hard time focusing on the story [Gil] taught it each night, even though the story seemed to rhyme. The accidental immigrant, who was from a place where all the different creatures enjoyed endless pleasure and self-knowledge, was crashing on boraxy speed, and his head was pounding. He felt dehydrated like never before and wondered where they'd get more speed for the long night ahead.

Also, because the short, square, elf-like captor was trying to impress the downstairs neighbors with fake ghetto-speak, the red wrinkly listener knew not to trust what she said much.

Free will just came, just like that, and the animal felt quite possessed and alone.

"Let winter come over us and bring us more of this wonderous ice, then I'll be great," thought the miserable knick-knack from his pillow, while my girlfriend stared into his tiny eye-nubs reciting hypnotic ballads of her youth:

I was a slut of thirteen.
My pops, he was to me mean.
I aborted his ill-gotten kid,
then ran off to Charleston and hid.
Now the cult men all chase me.
They're hasty – I'm tasty.
They all gave me AIDS.
I get straight A grades.

AND:

I'm three,
my mother's dead,
The Little Golden Book
half-read.
My wicked father

sneaks away,
I teach myself to
read that day.
The animals are happy
in the forest,
no one there is richest,
no one poorest.
So, mother smiles dead,
the story ends
then father fucks
and murders
all my friends.

NOT TO MENTION:

Tadahh!
I am the happy
spinning victim!
Watch me dancing
full of rage and sorrow!
Real tears roll as I,
myself, inflict them!
Same channel,
same tragedy tomorrow.

When she'd taught me the rhymes, I had memorized them right away. I acted out the parts for her immediately: the Father, the Mother, the Child, the Beast.

(No one had ever told me it could be that good – the never ever knowing. Identities switching from one body to the other, drawing all our pasts into one single eternal moment. Alone/All One. The father the mother the child the beast.)

Blinky told her, "I'll try to remember the legends, but I'll need a little something to help me stay up and practice. Can you recite the verses again?

She cut another line. Then she replied: "Every story is only clues. If the story appeals to you, it's certain you are one of the characters, and you may understand what your destiny holds. Oracles do no more than scroll through the possibilities they know and pick the one you fit best. You can do this for yourself. We know these stories because the stories and us are making each other, reiterating each other."

"These stories know us, too," somebody inside Blinky's head whispered.

"The only problem, Blinky, is when you doubt your own instinct. Then you need your so-called Enkidu for instinct. Everything else is lavender assembly-line Earth Goddesses who think they can get you all wrapped up in their long hair and then drop you down onto the sidewalk so they can pity you and feel empowered.

"Or everything is just wannabe goddesses, and that's whores. It's a gender revolution right now, Blinky, you know – 'I'll be the doctor and you be the patient, no I will, no I will…'

"I guess I look like a boy when I want to. It doesn't matter what forms we come in, it's like rearranging the molecules in ice-cream cones and rocking chairs in the end; it matters that I am boy-like and to be boy-like is to like boys and to have girls like you. The whores are sad and happy, up and down with whimsy, like kids. Their little emotions bubble up all over their faces. They want to be restrained but only when it's not against the law, because they do not like to break the law, like kids. Call it women's intuition of jail. That, I have in me, too.

"I'm like the best of both bad worlds. I've also got this lip-pierce that makes my girlfriends go crazy. Women and children – they like to suck and bite."

And then:

I wondered about her intentions.

She tattooed herself with the label and disclaimer "noble savage" as a way, I guess, to take the sting away, reclaiming this stupid term that hadn't been used in 200 years. Children, said Romantic Rousseau, were like the elegant primitive person. The beautiful-because-free-of-real-culture person.

But as far as I could tell, dykes who grew up in cults and who got knocked-up by their murderous fathers and who had debilitating mental illness plus genius and talent, who turned tricks in the tenderloin, did a lot of drugs, fucked their brother on occasion, and were HIV positive were not free of culture. They were not 'free.'

Likewise, Blinky wasn't a child, he wasn't a dyke, and he wasn't from any place near ancient Sumer. He never lived in any real forest, and he never sacrificed his life for [Gil]. He wasn't the fall-guy or the scapegoat, like Enkidu.

He lived, after all, and she died.

In *The Epic* Enkidu is a protective sidekick and a wound-trigger. His main purpose is to guard his friend and be a reflection of Gilgamesh's strength and might. His more enduring function is to die and be the object of Gilgamesh's suffering, his humanity. Enkidu shows Gilgamesh his soft, rotting wound – that is, his heart.

Femininity is wounded masculinity, all messy and open, all swampy and yearning. It can't protect the pursued.

I like it.

d that is the true

nobody wants us ry to enjoy.

y to see it. Being al performance- tims, that is one diers. Remember, ways does. There reams remember rld. Even if you are not being attacked by your government. Everything in you knows what happens when they need you but you also disgust them. It's a tricky ecosystem. It's like men and women or the whole world and Africa, parents and children or people and animals. It's been this slapstick battle for thousands of years. We've already read this story – so why are we bothering to read it now? I mean, we already know the ending, right?"

"Oh," the sidekick yawned.

[Gil] continued, "In the *Epic of Gilgamesh*, I don't know if I am looking for my Gilgamesh to replace my father, or if I am the Gilgamesh. If I am the Gilgamesh, I am looking for my Enkidu.

"He was a wildman, like you, Blinky, so if his forest is anything like my concrete jungle, we're in business. Those crack dealers downstairs are into smoking out – I'll bring them some hash oil and charm them."

For awhile [Gil] aligned herself with a particular Lower Haight brand of masculinity. She lived right up the hill from the Pink Palace, the most dangerous housing project in San Francisco. She hung out there with the guys from downstairs and played tough.

Stripping In The Underworld

In the small grove of cedars in the temple garden, Inanna began her story:

The gatekeeper opened the first gate suspiciously. He looked behind to see if anyone was following me. I told him I was alone. He said I had to give him my crown. I asked why. He said only, "The ways of the underworld are perfect. They may not be questioned."

I had sealed into my garments and gear the powers I had collected from my grandfather, the ones that made me omnipotent and kept me shielded and safe. I had transformed the abstract powers into tangible objects, and I wore them to keep them close at hand. The guard smirked at me. I could go back if I were afraid. I was a courageous warrior, so I gave him my crown. Just as soon as I handed over the crown, I lost several of my most valued powers.

Specifically, I lost access to the mysteries of walking, running, stealing away, cooling the heart, soothing, and fitful wandering. I also lost the power to destroy and to build, to lift up and to put down, and to turn man into woman and woman into man. I lost the forces of allure, ardent desire, and I could no longer control wealth, quick profits, indebtedness, or ruinous loss. These gifts I had taken I'd now given as toll.

My head felt overly light, as if it were filling with wind. Still I maintained my dignity. I followed the guard down a steep damp slope. I could hear the faint echoes of dripping. I could not see where we were going.

At the second stop the guard opened the gate and told me to go in, again, only if I had the courage. I went in.

He ripped away the primary beads at my neck. Furious, I demanded to know why. Again, he responded that the ways of the underworld were perfect and could not be questioned. In those beads was my power to teach, to watch over, to supervise and scrutinize. And in forfeiting the beads I also lost the keys to life vigor. I had no more control over guardian spirits or places of worship than any regular man.

There was a tightness in my throat that felt like venom swelling it shut, and my breath came out like panting. Still I maintained my calm.

At the third gate he took my double strand of red beads. Again he told me not to question why and dared me to turn back. I lost the ability to extend the word of rejection, the word of riddance, to hand out tender mercies to restore someone's broken heart, to control the trembling of the heart, weakness, shivering cramps and illness. A hot heaviness gathered like an electrical storm in my chest. My heart beat like a herd of escaping terrorized hooves on hard dirt. I knew the that I was dying.

A the fourth gate I was weaker and more confused. The guard said I could turn around and ascend any time. I hated him, and if I had kept my powers I would have crushed his skull against the stone wall.

He leered as he pried off my breastplate, and I did not have the strength to stop him. I had never experienced the sensation of violation before, but now my chest and stomach were bare, and I felt like a tender fawn with a broken leg.

In the absense of my armor, I lost the authority of granting a husband or a wife, of sparking a fight, of causing a person to be lazy or to tend with care. I was unable to remember how to build a house and furnish it or to bring a baby into the house. When my breastplate was seized, I lost all authority to give the royal crown and throne to kings, or to heap on lavish adornments. I could not grant cultic rites and guide their execution.

I had, for the first time in my life, no way to shield myself. I had lost the ability to win a fight.

I know now vulnerability is only the first phase of oblivion. I could no longer remember why I had chosen to leave all certainty behind. The guard continued to descend, and I could not stop myself. Or, I did not want to.

I followed.

December 14, 2006

Dear Winky,

Here, I'll show you the page in my old journal where I wrote that [Gil] shared needles with a guy who had the virus.

The writing is very matter-of-fact. I didn't know whether she was telling the truth or just being dramatic. I was worried, yes, but it didn't seem real.

I disgust myself.

Am I still someone who, in the same breath could write with such nonchalance that girlfriend had shared an HIV-infected needle and that I may have eaten a bug in my soup?

Jesus. I was just making a little comic spin. 'Cause it was no big deal because it was expected. What was unexpected was that bug. That was the big fucking surprise.

– Nina

Ha ha. Yikes. I think. Ha ha. I just ate a part. Of a bug. Ha ha. In my soup. Ha ha. Yikes. I think. I just ate a part. Ha ha. Of a bug.

Honestly she was so beautiful, her body is so small now [Krishna] shared a needle with her & is HIV+. He lied to her, told her he was not. The day she got high when [Mo] was in the hospital, that was the day. She shared a needle w/ a fag. His boyfriend is positive. [Krishna] looks sick as a dog.

She never put cold metal in my arm, the notion is not romantic at all, but sharp.
          Yikes I think I just ate part of
a bug in my soup.

Yikes.

. . . . he provided for his friend,
. . . . of his waist
. . . . he provided for his friend.
. . . . he provided for his friend.
. . . . he provided for his friend.
. . . . he provided for his friend.

its corpse he did throw down in the streets,
its innards he did throw down in the broad streets,   Ma 135

. . . . he provided for his friend.
. . . . of his waist
. . . . he provided for his friend.
. . . . he provided for his friend.
. . . . he provided for his friend.
. . . . he provided for his friend.   **Yikes.**

December 15, 2006

Winky,

I know this sounds crazy, but it seemed natural, that we'd all end up with AIDS. Just nature taking its course. Love to the virus, love to the plot.

How could I not be HIV-positive after all the guys I took home with me. Bisexual heroin addicts with long blue hair and girl-friends. Of course the virus was swimming wildly through me. I'd actually held an unwrapped condom in my hand the whole time I was fucking this hippie street musician I'd found on Telegraph. I held it there in my fist thinking, "I'm so fucking stupid."

In my unstewed reason, in my cocky sorrow, I thought I knew enough about grief to ignore it. But I didn't know grief.

What I knew was depression, numbness, despair and rage. I knew about rejection and being left to fend for myself.

I knew about wanting to die, and once about wanting to kill, but not about death.

No one I loved had died. So I knew a different kind of bereavement, the kind where you mourn the loss of the living, not the dead.

It's different. It's so fucking different.

—Nina

Ringgggg. Rinnnggggg.

Codewords for Fucked in the Forest Of Fucked

We said:

"I probably already have it. I'm sure I do."

"The only reason I'd want to know is so I won't pass it on."

"But I'm only with you, so who cares?"

"I probably have it already, too. You probably don't have it. You think you do?"

AIDS was laying itself down in beds, sucking on mints, pan-caking the sores on its face, holding out its hand. It went so far past overkill, it became a sparkling day of the dead, the campy apocalypse. Rich dykes were dipping themselves in black latex, like misshapen seals. Skin was off limits. Tasting the bitter grease between a woman's legs was like licking the ground in Chernobyl. Blood was off limits. But blood was so beautiful then, like a field of poppies, alive, just under the skin inside everyone.

Cuckoo, cuckoo.

You think you do?

As if there were a clock in the room and it was broken, going off five times every five minutes. Got it? You got it? Nah, I don't got it. Probably. Me, too. You think I got it? Nah. You? And it seemed inevitable, funny even, that I would be one of the ones who died and were blamed for their own deaths. It seemed I was put on the earth to enact that tale, the one everyone knows, faces shoved in it over and over, the shit morality story of beginnings, battles with self, and endings, all tidy like that, all moral.

I got wasted, threw myself into any warm touch, rolled over and bucked like some universe trying to form. I loved it, fucking strangers, sucking drugs and anything hard from the time I was 14 years old. I didn't care. What was better? Nothing. Life was meant to be lived, to suck, to slam. We were told to use condoms. Girls wore condoms head-to-toe. Dykes in San Francisco were starting to go wild with condom-like prophylactics for their tongues, their hands, thinking if boys were getting the disease, girls would, too. Thinking, if junkies and hookers and adulterers were getting the disease, girls would, too. Latex hysteria rattled us. We checked our hands for paper cuts, we vowed never to taste the juice of another cunt, it wasn't worth it, our time would come.

"Tested" was a code word. Tested meant tested for HIV. Tested meant caring whether you lived or died or killed. Tested couldn't mean anything else.

"Come here, let me hold you," [Gil] said, putting her meaty arms around my rib cage, her fingers against my back muscles.

"You don't have it, Pumpkin. You'd know it if you had it." Then, "You should get tested."

"I know, I know. I'm gonna. I really should. I haven't even been to the dentist in three years."

We had found each other in complete darkness, fingering Blinky, fingering clues. We could smell each other's suffering blood. Blood like the glowing waste in the tap water thrown out by some B-movie reptile God with a blade for a finger. I didn't have any use for that hateful politician God, not at all, that fucking father, that fucker, customer, waste of my time, that evil warlock who didn't exist.

[Gil] had a medicine cabinet with drugs in it to keep her calm, and AZT. She kept her hash in there, too.

"Never ever look in my cabinet," she said. And, like an asshole, I never did.

But she was convinced that I searched her things when she left the room, and that I knew all her secrets. Who else she was sleeping with. What she did when she went out at night, insomniac. Her diagnoses, her lies.

She believed I was fucking the customers at the peepshow after work on the side. I was such a little game-player. Trying to outwit her, trying to win.

"You're at risk with your job," she'd say.

"At risk" was what we called it. We flicked around code words like "tested" and "positive" and "sick."

"You go those guys at work, I know," [Gil] said. "You go somewhere with them, back to their car or up in some room?"

I wanted to be that girl, secretive and contained. But I wasn't. I told everything, confessed compulsively, hooking myself into my lover, hooking myself in and nesting there.

I would have been that girl, if I could. I'd have proven we were characters in the same tale together, pre-scripted, and necessary villains, angelic even, heroic monsters. She would have seen in my eyes what I knew: that the most contorted perversion was often the shortest distance between two breaking points. If I'd have been the lying whore I so wanted to be, I'd have convinced her we were together.

"You need to get tested," she said earnestly in the candlelit room, running her hand up my arm. She believed I was lying to her about what I did, who I was, what I knew. She believed I was cagey and brave. That was her love, and that's what I took.

"I know, I know, I will." I would. Sometime. Down at the Free Clinic, right down the street.

I put it on my list. Get tested, call the financial aid people again, write grandmother, read Bataille book by Wednesday, buy batteries.

I didn't know shit. It was all some big story I was reading, all some drama with shifting proscenia, mono-logues, fast costume changes. All some big story I was transcribing. Looking for clues, digging for prompts.

The tragic climax was coming, I knew. All the stars with knives in their chests, the crescendo, the flopping about on the floor, with blocking marked out in mask-ing tape X's. It was the best part of the whole opera.

I thought I was a character. I didn't know I was alive.

Why doesn't anyone answer the fucking phone?

The City of Empty Pounding Fists

The city was filling up with empty holes where bodies once were, holes that stood-in for corpses and holes for the ones crying over them, wives and boyfriends fighting over the stick-figure hole, parents dressing it up in suits and Easter dresses, pulling their hole grimaces into soap commercial smiles or burning the holes, dismissively, long distance.

The gruesome slaughter seemed completely normal, just another moment in history, because history itself was a big blockbuster propaganda fest all set up by whoever did the most killing.

Had I known about resistance then, I might not have caved to history, but those stories are jealously guarded. The defense I knew was to hide, disdain, shout curses from my cave, get high and crawl into bed.

Many others all over the world were fighting. They believed they might be heard, that they mattered enough to be heard. They found each other, railed for justice. Revenge. Witness.

It was the right thing to do.

They sat in folding chairs around Formica tables in church basements, smearing eyeliner, gentle press of stranger's hand to stranger's shoulder. Made dirty jokes into accusing chants. Loved loud, pissed in public, and rioted in sequins against the inevitability of the enemy always winning.

Dykes did it. Whores, too, and art dealers, thin men with scabs. Women who'd lost no lovers did it. Raged with each other, fought.

They demanded more money be put into AIDS research. That the new drugs be put on the market and made affordable. That doctors stop treating the sick like they were at fault. That lovers be given the right to sit with their partners as they coughed in hospital rooms and watched *Days of Our Lives* turned down low.

December 23, 2006

Dear Winky,

   I didn't fight. Wasn't a "joiner." Didn't believe that anything but weapons and money changed shit. Didn't know about offering support, didn't know about community. Didn't feel entitled to health and fair treatment. Didn't think that when they said "people" they were talking about me. Never expected help or to help. Never knew. Truly had no idea.

   Plus I was busy, way too busy. On my own, ambitious. Trying to finish school, learn a trade, leave the country. Go to Prague. Join the former revolutionaries, the wooden puppet-makers. Join something else.

   Find that enchanted elsewhere with its sexy elsewhere worries, and dissolve there like a wish.

                                                        Nina

Caregiver and Carrion

"Angela told me all the professors who are so worried about me ARE DEFINITELY vultures, but that caring about people isn't bad faith!" [Gil] whispered, gleeful but sober, grabbing my arm in the hallway before Anti-Psychiatry class.

Angela was the Anti-Psychiatry professor as well as Gil's new therapist. [Gil] was so happy, she was so relieved. She was so thin. At break I found her in the lobby, curled in a loveseat, wearing my leather jacket. I was leaving. I needed my coat.

"Nope," I said. Her skin was grey-green. "Give it. I have to go."

She raised the armholes, I peeped down them. Her wrists were cut. She was bleeding on my jacket, where the liner was frayed and greasy. "Give it to me. I don't care."

[Gil] knew about girls like me, we were a type. Our sexuality wasn't about gender. We loved the wounded come-back kids who made us laugh. I cared, I cared so much it scared me. Caring's not always bad faith, but sometimes it is. Sometimes it's all about the one seeming to care, not the one needing care.

Fuck it. I didn't want to care anymore. I was so sick of responding to her manipulative little pleas, so embarrassed to find myself being that easy target hooker with a heart of gold who gives away all her earnings kind of girl. I hated the obvious. I left. She found some bandages and wrapped her stupid wrists.

Do you think she cared for something? Do you think she could? If she was not herself, who was? Who was there to feel compassion? Is compassion the same thing as caring? Do you think she felt compassion? Do you think she could?

Tell me.

She cared for Sylvia Plath and Ted Berrigan. And the guys who sold her cocaine downstairs.

She cared for a couple of poetry professors and her ex girlfriend, Mo.

And she cared for Blinky, her sidekick.

December 31, 2006

Dear Winky,

Happy New Year. Also: Don't get frustrated. Just listen. This is too important to turn into fable. You'll need to know all this shit by heart before you leave, and it's almost time for you to go.

Maybe where you come from, there's a nondiscursive certainty, a kind of animal instinct, a nature that isn't made up. But where you're going to is the world of representations that even direct experience become, once you think about it or put it into words. It makes everything into a story. And stories have the nasty side-effect of casting a shadow over all other latent stories.

I'm not saying stop believing you're a girl or a boy or a human with a human spirit or a woodland creature. I'm saying no matter what you make up, it's received wisdom. I'm saying you are a beautiful unique conglomeration of everyone else's desires including those that feel unique to you.

I'm saying opposites don't cancel each other out. The world of representations is a world of illusions, so it couldn't hurt too much to delude yourself more interestingly.

I'm not saying truths are relative. Strange-ify received definitions, that's what I'm saying. Look at every thing askance – tilt your head, lift your trunk and sniff. Feel it out with your quantum heart strings, which adore the surreal.

Again, I'm not saying the oil company never killed its striking workers using hired mercenaries and importing other workers from refugee camps. I'm not saying that's not true, or morally relative. I'm not saying maybe all the girls who got raped and otherwise violated by their dads, uncles, brothers, cousins, teachers, coaches, grandpas and family friends are remembering a dream instead of a fact. I'm not saying equal protection extends to those not needing protection. I'm not saying facts aren't experienced. And I'm not saying there're no absolutes.

I'm talking about belief. I'm wondering about it, and I'm saying it. I'm saying the effects of various beliefs exist as truth, for instance, human rights or the idea "enemy."

I'm saying stories exist as truth and make beliefs real.

I'm saying change the way you tell yourself stories starting with the characters, starting with the idea of what a character can be. Just check it out. Just for a kick.

Does a character have to have one identity, is that its definition? Does it have one motive, one history, one psychology? Is it doomed or blessed because of its one intention? Is the ending already written? This idea of character comes from an individualist paradigm. It's the basis of contemporary moral categories of agency, autonomy, and personal responsibility. Coherence of self is the foundation of law. Did she attempt to murder or didn't she? Is she guilty or not?

Both. Neither. When you say "she," what do you mean?

In Synopology's view, everyone's possessed by thousands of Zzzatans, so everyone's a composite of disgruntled souls. That doesn't seem far-fetched to me. It's like the inverse of communal. Think of Anti-Oedipus. A flock of desiring I-machines. Synopology was a post-bomb religion. Scabbard understood that people felt uncomfortably multiple, especially French philosophers and the Americans who read them. Scabbard knew Americans in the 1950s needed to feel unified and self-contained, and he knew they wanted to be monitored. They were so afraid of fascism, they signed up for oligarchy.

Here's a story your basic TV-watcher is pretty familiar with: Fucked up daughter of half-assed cult leader gets brutalized, body, heart and mind. She runs away to the City, turns tricks, gets betrayed after extending the tiniest bit of trust, grows even more disenchanted, uses needles, couple of rapes. Gets a burst of survival instinct, goes to college, learns ancient languages, scores big with the girls, writes some devastating and insightful poems, gets AIDS, goes crazy, dies alone in violence and shame.

How predictable. Like cops and robbers. Or a crumbling blue-water yellow-sand epic. Losers lose, survivors survive. The hero always wins. That's what makes him the hero, winning. It's another tautology.

And the tragic hero, he almost wins. Again, "almost" defines tragedy. He thinks he'll win, and everyone hopes he'll overcome his obstacles and tragic flaws, but it's pretty likely he's going

to get AIDS and end up stuck in a hospital bed hooked up to tubes before he kills himself the way he wants.

We've seen this story before. We know how to read the signs. It doesn't take a rocket scientist or a Roland Barthes. If it's in the "News" part of the newspaper or a Japanese film, the tragic hero kills himself. But if it's on the big screen at the mall multiplex, he finds a woman or a pet to stand by him through various predictable difficulties while he eventually seeks recovery from his addictions and freedom from his demons, and then he and the woman are standing in the very clean kitchen of the new house of their new life looking out the window. Maybe a child laughs or a bird flies.

If the director is trying to be especially cunning, maybe there's a minute where the audience wonders if they're watching a comedy. They might feel a tiny shock of hope when the raped fucked-up dyke starts getting some attention for her poetry and her intellect, when the love interest accepts the hero for who she really is, really deep down, beautiful and bright and wild, before all the mind-torquing and torture. Which of course means the beautiful love interest loves a woman who never existed, even in the past, since there was no before. Which means she isn't really loving. Which means this can't be a comedy. It has to be a tragedy.

It's a story that's like a self-fulfilling prophecy, which if it weren't, it wouldn't get told. Or at least not told and retold.

Which came first, Winky, the disempowered lightening man or his disempowered cyclone mother? His hidden bloody rags, or the little girl's plastic tiara? Which came first, the guy who thinks he might just want to set up a new religion or the daughter who condemns him lyrically but kills herself physically to become a rebellious hero, not another boring psychopath's daughter?

I'm saying these predictable storylines make for predictable tragedies. I'm saying it's an ancient part of the mind that works in allusion. I'm saying stop believing in language and see what it's like to experience the horrifying peacefulness of not waiting for the cue.

Love,
Nina

Truthbearing Conventions

Before Blinky found himself disoriented, lying on his side in the gutter on the corner of Page and Payne, he had been dreaming. It was the kind of hibernation dream that happened throughout the season, a transformative tale and the real reason behind hibernation in the sparkling overstocked forest.

In his dream, a wild and crazy welcome butterfly with rainbow shoestrings fluttered in circles on one wing, the other having fallen to shreds. The butterfly was saying, "It's time to wake up, it's time to wake up!"

So Blinky did wake up and the butterfly said, "Watch out for the goose!"

Blinky said, "You are mistaken, there is no goose. Also, you appear to be in your final moments of life, so I greatly appreciate your choice to spend them in duty and friendship with me.

The butterfly responded, "Oh, but there is always a goose. And I am not dying yet. First I have a fun lesson for you – one that will make your life meaningful."

At which point Blinky began to wonder whether he were really awake. Something was not adding up. Sleeping was for lessons, not waking. Waking was for commerce. Was the butterfly lying?

How could a truthful lesson be born from a lie?

"A myth," honked the goose who was Time and therefore invisible. A sequence of prompts chained together to create a physiological and conceptual experience. Or to recreate one more slowly.

In this dream, in the voice of a philosopher, Blinky said, "Lying is a perversion of our language and it messes up communities by undermining trust. It steals choice from the one who receives it by giving them a false choice and treating them like objects only there for the liar's own ends."

The goose laughed. She said, "A lie is in the eye!" She coughed and the lights went out in the cave.

The butterfly finished, "A lie is in the eye of the beholder. A lie is determined by intention. Intention is buried in selfhood. Selfhood is contingent upon a sense of solidity and separation. Senses are notoriously ambiguous. For instance, it may seem to you that you hear something in the background. Something ringing."

"I do. Is it my alarm clock ringing?"

The goose said, "It is an alarm of sorts. But you're already awake. And dreaming, too." And she laughed more sadly. "That's what I mean about lying. I mean both 'yes' and 'no.'" Then she said, "I'll hit snooze, so you can wake up slowly." The ringing stopped.

"I don't get what you're trying to teach me. I don't understand the riddle." He got on all four legs and rubbed his eyes with his trunk. The lights flickered back on, as if there were a storm raging outside.

"Are you saying I am not who I think I am? That 'I' am contingent upon others' experience of me, but trapped with only one experience of myself?

"If you're trying to tell me I lack a solid self, I want my money back on this dream. Because I've already had that lesson and it gets me nowhere. It doesn't help anyone and it's not funny."

To which the butterfly, now almost entirely wingless

and scarred said, "Get your mittens, your little hat. Follow me to the burned-out patch of bones where I'm heading to lay myself down. Bury yourself under the ash and go back to sleep. A ringing sound will wake you. Answer the call, which will be a dangerous threat. Nonetheless, pick up the phone. You will find yourself in the City, which is only a forest with amnesia. When you wake, you won't remember a thing."

The Red Light of The Sacred

I was in my booth at The Kingdom. I hadn't heard from [Gil] in three days. She'd disappeared. Maybe she was dead. Nobody knew where she was. Whatever. She was so tortured, why shouldn't she kill herself? She should do it if she wanted. Maybe it was the best thing for her. The world would go on.

I was in my booth in between customers, wondering if I'd kill myself, too, maybe that night, why not? I was cutting a line of yellow-tooth speed with the knife I had first fucked [Gil] with, keeping my index finger over the blade.

There were times it didn't hurt to be alive, I reminded myself. There was always a war somewhere in the world where people had way more to be miserable about than me. And in the projects. And children.

You should write this all down, I told myself. But I couldn't write. I had been up for two days and a night. Hardly anyone was coming in to my booth. I couldn't think of anyone in the world I could talk to but [Gil]. Why would anyone stay alive by choice? My mother wanted to kill herself. My best friend wanted to die and often seemed dead. I wanted to die. [Gil] wanted to die. The only people I knew who didn't want to die

were dumb people and mean people. As far as I could see you could either be stupid, cruel, or suicidal.

So what was the big deal? Do it if you want to do it.

I was trying to get drunk on Smirnoff and orange juice. It was around nine in the morning and nobody was coming into my booth. I needed money and felt like shit. I looked like shit. I was crashing. I hated speed. Once you started doing it you had to keep doing it until you had enough time and some pills for the crash.

I didn't want to open the window to my booth and see the men walk by. I hated them. I hated this. I wished I were religious so I could pray. I used to believe in something. I wanted to believe in something. I was just crashing, that's all. I did a burning line. I smoked a cigarette and blew the smoke into the fan. I wished I believed. Maybe that's what was coming next for me, some kind of spiritual thing.

But what was the point in getting a god? It was all bullshit. What was the point? A customer knocked on my window and I didn't answer. I hated them. I hated this. I was ugly. Everything was ugly, the fake brass chandelier and headboard, my thighs, the ash on the rug, my teeth. Everything was ugly in the world and I wanted to die.

If I became spiritual, some sort of goddess worshipper or something like that, I'd have something to pray to when I was crashing. I'd feel comforted. And that was bullshit, that was just me convincing myself to keep living. And I wanted to die. So I prayed. I said, "Inanna or whoever, I know you're not real and you know I don't believe in anything and I want to die and I hurt so bad and everything in the world is so fucked up I just want to kill myself, I want to kill myself, I can't stand living, it's so fucking pointless."

And I heard, "You don't want to die. You just want everything to be different. There's a difference." I heard the voice in my head, like thought. It was totally right. I was stunned.

I didn't have this urgent desire to be dead. What I wanted was for people to stop hurting each other and using each other and fucking up the planet. I wanted everyone to be able to go to school without working at the peepshow, and for people to stop selling crack. I wanted everyone to have enough to eat and for it to be delicious. I wanted the politicians to admit they'd been lying selfish shits and hand the government over to kind honest people. I wanted those kind people to offer reparation for slavery and imperialist conquest.

I wanted men to stop hurting women and women to stop hurting children. All of it. All the regular normal shit to want. I wanted things to change. I wanted the government to stop giving money to dictators to squash righteous rebellion. I wanted people to stop cheating on each other. I wanted my mother to be strong enough apologize. I wanted everyone to have somewhere to live and someone who loved them. I wanted all the suffering to end all over the world. It didn't matter that it wasn't possible. What mattered at that moment was that I wanted it, that I wanted at all.

I didn't want to die. I wanted things to change. There was a difference.

Maybe [Gil] didn't really want to die either. Maybe we all just wanted things to be different. Maybe that's why it felt so horrible that she was going to kill herself, because it wasn't what she really wanted. It was like a booby prize.

There I sat in my booth, high, cross-legged on my fake bed with traces of meth on window ledge where I kept my dildos and lube. My forehead was wet and my eyes were welling. Holy shit, I thought, blowing smoke up into the spinning fan.

Holy shit.

The Seventh Veil

I stood on the threshold of the fifth gate, not knowing what to do. The guard pointed to my gold ring. To utter slander, words of deception, to speak unashamedly, even hostilely, to sneer at an answer false or true, to say wicked words had been mine in that ring. To joke, inflame a quarrel, provoke laughter, to defile, to esteem. My center was made of bubbling tar where animals screamed as they drowned. My head buzzed with thoughts of turning around, I had learned enough. To continue was impossible. I was prepared to surrender.

"I want to go back," I said to the guard.

"It's too late for that," he replied. You're nearly at the bottom.

The gates behind me were locked, but even if they had been open, I had no strength to run. This was the wisdom of no escape. It hurt beyond description. I vomited on the 6th gate.

My body was not my own anymore. The gatekeeper easily took my lapis measuring rod. I couldn't discern right from wrong or any other distances of measure. I knew the feeling, but not the bases of calamity, bitter woe, torment, evil, fear, panic, alarm. I could no longer stifle terror, trembling sickness, and sleeplessness, nor cause a dreadful brilliance or strike or slaughter. I could not raise the battle cry. There was no fight left whatsoever.

At the 7th gate, my royal robe was removed, and I barely noticed. I was no longer myself. I was without will or discernment. I could make nothing safe or indestructable. I could not get revenge or imprison the enemy. I was not all knowing. I could not set anyone free.

The gatekeeper locked the gate behind me. He stayed on the other side. He handed my things through the bars to a servant. He did not continue to taunt me. He looked at me with pity.

I dragged my naked body, human and bruised, into the throne room to face my sister. It crossed my mind that the humilliation and suffering would soon be over.

I had experienced complete loss of myself. It felt horrifying and then it felt just.

The judges of the underworld surrounded me. I recognized many of them from another time. Not recognizing me as a goddess they judged me ready for death.

I was stunned, if that's possible. This was not death. I had not yet experienced death.

November 12, 1992

Tonight after my Russian lesson I found out from Maria that [Gil] had fallen or jumped off a roof at school and was found by someone. I couldn't get the number of where she is staying. Last night after I got home from work I took a bath and used my new cock to fuck myself, then I went to sleep. I slept and woke and slept and woke and slept and woke. All night and morning with both lights on. Each time I woke I felt wide awake but didn't want to move.

It was scary on Monday when I couldn't keep myself from going back to her house even though she choked me the night before Halloween. I was sitting at the bus stop at midnight watching myself go to her and wondering why I couldn't stop myself, just watching like I was in a fucking movie. All of a sudden I'm not worried about her, I'm worried about me.

It is curious this distance I feel from [Gil]'s recent events, jumping off the bridge, the roof, the paranoia, the possible cheating, the drugs. I don't feel like I am consciously pushing emotions away, either. I don't feel drugged. I don't feel like it happened in a book or in a far-off land. I don't feel that pseudo vampiric intrigue like it happened to someone I've heard about but only makes me think about myself. Maybe she will never call me again. Maybe she'll come over and want to sleep with me tonight. And I'll let her in.

This drama is SOOOO FUCKING INSANE.

Anna Joy Springer

Warning!

On the Thursday evening following [Gil]'s suicide attempt, an older poet from Alternative University got the number from the school records and phoned. It was the first time anyone from the school had called to talk about [Gil].

"Look little girl, I know this girl you've been fucking around with. I've been with her in the hospital and I saw the charts."

THEN:

"I know what she did to her last girlfriends, and she's doing it to you, too."

FOLLOWED BY:

"Get away. Run away as fast as you can into the dark woods at the edge of town, into the forest the colonists despise. Run to the devils, the fierce animals and holes for your snapping ankles. Hold out your soul in your hands before you as you run, and offer it to the demons for the price of your stay, because there it is far safer than if you were to run to her."

November 13, 1992

All the great dangers threatening humanity with extinction are direct consequences of conceptual or abstract thinking.

I need to get off, but I can't. I've been masturbating two hours already.

Fuck the Enlightenment.

Stuck In Time, Mortality Becomes An Issue

It was foggy and cold when Blinky stepped out of his cave, onto the street, awake, braced. He met an unfriendly rat who accused him of volition. He met a sidewalk who wouldn't say a word, and couldn't walk, swim, or fly. It could not replicate or rot. It was neither alive nor dead.

In the past: Life and death, happily well-groomed animals and coquettish suns circling the forest floors with suave, flirtatious assurance, winter diamonds sparkling tenaciously, baby animals born warm, underground. This according to [Gil], who'd created her sidekick's origin myth.

"But then, Time couldn't bear the loneliness anymore," [Gil] instructed her new friend. "'Cause it was cursed by an evil witch due to jealousy, ego-training, whatever, some lack, post-separation from matter, mother, whatever, you get what I mean. So then Time made himself sticky, covering his limbs with a white substance vomited up by special insects.

"Time used this glue to attract company because Time grew bored of being abstract all alone. So, lonely and cunning in the forest, Time stuck to you, Blinky, then you were born, and then you were you! Without prompting, you and all the other animals burst into song, cause stuck in Time, you could finally hear yourselves and you could hear each other too!"

I'll jump in with my own interpretation about the origin of narrative. Imagine this:

Also, accidentally, stuck to Time was a goose who spoke only in annoying rhymes. That the rhymes became annoying to even the impossibly content animals of the forest is testament to the fact of a death instinct. Even the universe, which is expanding so fast it makes your head spin, is bound by its contract with Time.

And telling me about herself, [Gil] said, "I always know what women want. It's uncanny. Just one kiss, that's all it takes, and then I know, I can just feel it, I'm so sensitive that way, knowing how any girl wants it, that's how I know what you want, and I do know what you want, don't I? I do."

I stared at her lower lip ring.

"Even when I don't know that I know, I just know, it's like a body memory. My first shrink, when I got away from the compound and they put me in this home for runaways, I was thirteen or fourteen, she showed me. I never told you this before. She was my first girlfriend. She said I was made for loving women. She was my first, and I was a natural. She got me out of the home, and I moved in with her. She loved me. But I had to leave so she wouldn't get fired."

I think it was my own voice I heard in my sleep, all those echoes, I don't know, not hers. I awoke one day with a girlfriend, a dyke. She'd wrapped her leg around mine during a lecture about nature. I'd been coloring in my tattoo with wet watercolor pencils I licked and she pulled my leg out from under me, held it in between her boots, so I had to listen.

"Nature! Nature, instinct, we're killing Her,"

the misogynist professor read from his notes.

"But does anybody even try to see what I want? Does anybody know what I need like I know what they

need?" [Gil] demanded.

She wouldn't tell me about all the things she needed; she couldn't, so how could I know? Instead, she explained the concept of spiritual death to me.

Finally.

Now that I know what that humming is, I can use it to look forward to silence, when it comes, unannounced.

Or when I egg it on.

"So, Time split up into gazillions of pieces and moved away to all corners of the world, because everything that stuck to it began to bicker, and Time found its own consciousness unbearable," she finished.

That's how the tiny crafted elephant-like monster found itself in the City, where we struggled to wake up and loved.

From an Old Whore to a Young One

But before Blinky even realized he had an actual "will of his own," the dying elf-like woman captured him and made Blinky safe in her pocket.

They spent their afternoons smoking crack in the downstairs apartment at the corner of Page and Payne. I don't know if she was cheating on me or what, with one of those guys. She didn't have any money as far as I knew. They'd already cut off her Disability checks and she was too ugly, I thought, too boy-like, to turn tricks.

"I was up in the Carlton one time and I was supposed to let this Doberman fuck me, only once though, for a thousand bucks, and all these suits were watching, standing around in a circle, and I was in the middle with this dog, but it couldn't get its dick in, so I just sucked him off instead, and they let me keep all the money."

I must have looked impressed.

"You like that story?"

A suite in the Carlton or a gang-rape in a doorway; one of several, or just shooting up with friends, trustworthy friends, I understood. We did what we did because we had to, because it's the kind of thing we could do. She was not to be trusted but not totally mistrusted either, so I reverted to what I knew, and all I knew was that I did, I did like the story.

With the thousand dollars, she bought her ex-girlfriend a pair of blue cowgirl boots with dice on the ankles, and she paid some tuition at college, and then the dog-money was gone.

So, I don't know if my girlfriend was fucking those guys for the crack, using her incredible mouth on the boys with the crack. She started talking like she'd been there in the neighborhood all her life, but I knew she'd come from a planned cult community somewhere in the mountains of Virginia. And that overnight, her father would add new rooms to the house, while she was sleeping, so that in the morning, when she walked down a hallway, it would lead to a different room, and her father would be waiting there, in a crevice in the hallway, and he'd jump out to scare her on purpose.

I asked her, "How did he build a whole new addition to the house overnight?" and she said, "He just did."

"Yesssss," said the frenetic little Blinky, thinking aloud. The small animal was more maroon or wine-colored than red, only red in his crinkles. He was about the size of any tweak-toy you'd find on a street corner waiting for the forest to kick in. He was changing shape, getting flat. He had changed so much since she'd found him.

"Yessss, you can see the mutation while its happening," he muttered, "Jennnniferrrr."

If you stay awake, there it is. It's a choice, up the hill or down the hill, toward the Soul Food or toward the Shoe Shops, righty-tighty or lefty-loosey. Even mutation depends on artful engineers to arrange its fragments and functions.

The ugly elephant-like thing may have loved my dying girlfriend, but how could he have loved her like me? He did seem to enjoy the cocaine, that was the love, the way it made him talk so profound. He liked the burning plastic smell of the rock when it sizzled and gasped in the glass chamber of the pipe. I hated it.

(You want to see me put my head in the oven for dinner, give me cocaine. You want to see me listen too hard, agree myself into rugburn, cry and beg, and all that? Just light me up an idiot rock. If it's free. If it smells good.)

Gil was just the opposite of animal. Not a dirty little digger like me. She always hit the ashtray with her ash with honed precision. When the landlord found her dead on her mattress she'd just turned 31. She was a Virgo, a tidy brilliant earth sign. All her rings were lined up in alphabetical order on the night stand, and they were dead, too. Big giant silver butch dial-a-dad fuckrings from the flea market. Sensitive, she'd turned off the heat in the small dark apartment on 21st and Valencia, before she shot herself up, so that when she was dead, the cool summer fog would keep her corpse from rotting the sheets.

"Die Young and stay pretty!"

she'd joked, all the time.

"Are you talking about me or you?" I, the pretty one, laughed.

What Do You Mean By "Father"?

There's a difference between schizophrenia, like my father had, and multiple personalities, like [Gil] had, but people mix up the terms all the time.

We say, "Oh, I'm in a million different places at once, I'm not here, I'm so schizophrenic," or we say, "Capitalism makes everybody schizophrenic."

We don't mean we're hearing instructions and comments yelled into our ears, off stage. I like schizophrenics, but they make me lonely. What we mean is we feel at odds with ourselves or torn. Our consciousness strays hither and thither looking for something to land on.

There's a difference between schizophrenia and MPD, but people say the pattern of my love is as simple as houndstooth. My motivation carved in stone by the time I held my father's leg, simple as all that. There's chapters, even whole books on the way I love, you can read all about it. It's simple.

I'll never know if [Gil] heard voices or saw phantoms, for real, or if she was tricking me. To get me to study her or to give her comfort. To watch me follow the dance-steps painted on the floor, watch me falter, try again. Maybe she was like that.

[Gil] put my fist inside her. And that's how I learned about passive aggression. She inspected the little turkey-pink dick I bought and gave me a mama-kitty smile. Held her hips up in the air and gave me my choice, and then I was him. Him.

Whichever father, her own or God, the word, or the wildest wolf of the forest, him, that thing that stabs, that wounds, that moves like some blinking baby predator, feeding, inside a girl. Was I preconditioned to be a hero?

I wasn't scared of her. I wasn't scared of anything wild. Nothing would be harmed. All the semi-trucks would swerve gently, missing the baby crawling across the road at night, everything would swim in schools.

I learned how delightful it was to hurt something sweet. The cheaper the candy, the warmer the groove.

Organs, full of blood struggle and waste, made of meat, I thought of heating them in the microwave, then rolling in them and letting my bones make the organs pop open, how smooth, how slippery, some rugged extension of a soapy shaved leg in a tub, fatty like metaphor.

All these beautiful sensations from outer space, from dust. I was no regular girl anymore, I was feral, I was torn.

Before he left the wilderness, Enkidu put his beautiful stiff prick between the thighs of the long-haired whore. She held onto his balls, underneath, and pulled his leathery sac to bring him forward, slow and steady. She licked between the hairs. It felt to him like it feels to me at the crease between my pussy and thigh, where the large tendon throbs, when that place gets licked, slowly, slow and heavy like a burglar's hand on a doorknob. It felt like whose body's whose? Yeah.

That's how the whore licked Enkidu's balls. And let go of them, popping his gorgeous prick into her mouth and padding her teeth with her lips, and squeezing her

lips all the way up. It was all sorts of desperate flower shades, so she held Enkidu's balls a little tight to keep him from coming, then pulled her mouth off, so he opened his eyes.

She said, "There is this man. An evil, tyrannical man."

He didn't know what she was saying. He couldn't understand a word.

She said, "You don't know what I'm saying." So she cupped his face in her hands and ran her fingers over his uncursed mouth. "I will teach you."

In this scene which of the two was I? I was not the whore. It's who I thought I was, but I wasn't her yet. And I wasn't Enkidu, either.

I was not Gilgamesh, despite my martyring heroics. I was not fierce Inanna who put her beloved to death then brought him to life every year.

It's possible I was Inanna's servant. If I was anyone at all. The devoted one, waiting on the one with the power I loved to be near. The hottest woman in the universe, the smartest, toughest, and trickiest, would teach me and tame me like the whore did Enkidu.

But nobody would take that on, not wholeheartedly. So I had to do it myself.

Unlikely Witness

My sister stretched open her wide yellow eye and gave me a curdling look.

"So, little seeker," she said. "Now you're no Goddess of Heaven and Earth. Not even human, not even goat. Your self sits in pieces in that sack by the gate. All fashion and magic tricks. What you see now is what you were all along. A creeping thing no one could see beyond all the glitzy posturing. Now no one would feed you if they could see you. They would step over your stinking body in the street where it would lay while you starved slowly."

She seemed bitter. I had not expected that, I don't know why. I had expected a teacher.

Ereshkigal continued, "I know you think you'll be going home soon. But no one will bother to rescue you now. All you were to them was a uniform and a bag of gold. You aren't even as important as a fly now. There's your greatest wisdom. There's your grail. Drink from it, sister. I've held this Truth for years, and it's boring. There is one last thing you'll do tonight before you finally sleep."

I asked, "What more could there be?"

Ereshkigal said, "Now you will take off your flesh."

I found myself begging aloud to no one in particular, repeating "please" and "no" like a little boy.

But unfathomably, in a part of my mind, I remained curious. I flushed with shame and fear and could not make myself rise up off my knees.

<u>HOW WE ARE DIFFERENT.</u>

She is afraid she will be killed and I am afraid I'm too unimportant to die.

I dont care if she kills me, it would be a surprise & partly my fault.

**There are so many
ways to fight.**

January 2, 2007

Dear Winky,

Over and over, this obsession with the possibility that [Gil] would try to kill me. Did you ever worry for yourself?

She worried she would become a woman. And if she became a woman like me, one who felt her skin, one who genuflexed in a thousand tricky gestures, one who watched the watchers watching, she'd have no choice but to marry a man like her father, to be killed by him like her mother was.

It never occurred to her that she might become like her father. Because destiny is destiny, and history repeats itself, and behind every great man, there's a dumbass woman freezing, pleasing, appeasing.

But she became soft with me.

Winky, I knew you were not like me from the beginning. You never lost focus. I brought her back to her body, she said. But you helped her get away. So do it. Please. Go.

I'll miss you so much,

Nina

Meglomaniacal Rapture Flash

Could it have been with anyone, anyone of those artful sex fiends who loved jumping sci-fi worlds as much as I did? Who loved teaching, turning, as much as I did, who would go out on limbs toward grotesqueries of remorse, whose strong hands knew a body intuitively, and knew the mind as a tender empty shadow?

All over town in beds, scraped palms against brick walls, on bathroom floors, bubbling in cloudy hot tubs, poison, brooding, smoky, upsetting, ill, cumming like the end of the world. Were any beds so desperate, so clinging and impossible to stop like gravity, like shame, as ours?

She took me, with care and sometimes with disdain. She knew what would weaken me. I never understood more than she did, even if she understood everything wrong. She said I brought her back to her body. Her woman's body with tits and holes.

Touching her with my bittersweet hands she leaked. I was not trying to win.

But to her mind, all love interactions were a delicately sublimated battle of wills. Gifts with fishhooks like Halloween apples. Not a mutual flowering, but a struggle, all of it, coated in piss or bliss with clear winner and loser, known to both, but never acknowledged. Or, the acknowledgement saved for just the right time.

Did I win? She died and I lived.

So who I was melted into who I became and time stretched out for me, a little baggy and comfortably worn. I've never liked winning but like to brag, and maybe that's what I'm doing now. Do you know all your own intentions? I don't.

In her red bed, I found myself staring into the cool dark cave of myself, not knowing shit. My own voice echoing back like the one I sent out, telling me nothing new.

There was no way for me to prove my motives to myself or anyone. She placed in me a kettle of wriggling doubt. I could summon up pure cruelty, in our theater of sex.

And she made my guilty sadism gorgeous, turning the lights red and passing a line. I put my hand into her too hard, then purple blood fell out of her, and she said keep going. Like a hero.

My mind focused sharp, cut out all the words. I wasn't trying. I was free. I put my mouth in her blood and drank like some four-legged thing with dirty fur. And a gleaming phallus rose up quivering inside my chest like a song. Out of nowhere, bam.

Then, she was pissed. "Why did you keep going?" she asked.

I had hurt her cervix for real and was obviously only pretending not to notice.

I was like everyone else, trying to hurt her, trying to win. Maybe she was right. She died, I lived.

There were only two roles to take in the world. Femininity meant pretending to be under the thumb while trying to get the upper hand.

Masculinity meant pretending never to want to lose. So that suicide was masculine. So that when [Gil] killed herself, she became a man and no one could get her then.

Anna Joy Springer

The Perfect Cut

The butcher came and sliced away my skin, which curled in his hand like a hair.

I heard, then listened, to my own screaming, and it scared me. It scared me still more to be interested.

The butcher cut carefully. Almost lovingly. I wondered what kind of man he had been, and what had brought him to this vocation. His hands were very steady, and there was a thick bronze ring on his finger. Somebody cared for him.

He sliced off my hide in one whole piece, perfect. I watched.

I fell away from myself, excruciatingly conscious. In two places at once, I observed the drama of my dying, I observed the unbearable pain.

Still not dead, I watched the butcher fold my limp coat of flesh neatly.

Whatever was watching would have cried if it'd had a body. It trembled, longing to cry.

I wondered if my sister and the butcher could feel this enormous sorrow. There was a warmth to it, and I was comforted.

Slowly I unspiraled into a looser emptiness.

January 4, 2007

    So now, Winky, it's time.
    I plant you, my wadded-up seed, you piece of bullshit garbage that'll take a thousand years to decompose.
    Go.
    Go on.
    I send you with love.
    You're nothing.
    Become alive again and grow.

                    Your friend,
                    Nina

Pick up anything
for it may be the phone.

Anna Joy Springer

"What is a girl who disappears,
red, into a forest?"

- Bhanu Kapil

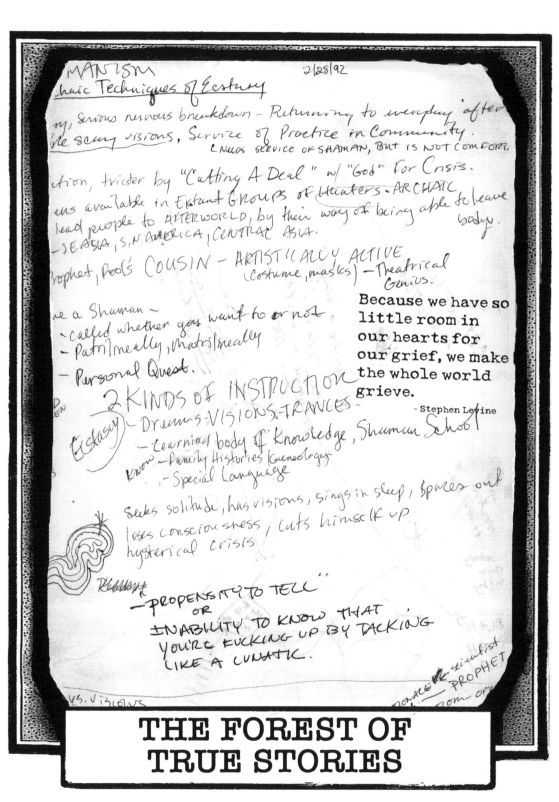

MAN?SM

2/28/92

haic Techniques of Ecstasy

ny, Serious nervous breakdown - Returning to everyday 'after
the scary visions, Service of Practice in Community.

↳ NEEDS SERVICE OF SHAMAN, BUT IS NOT COMFORT.

tion, trickster by "Cutting A Deal" w/ "God" For Crisis.

ens available in Extant GROUPS of Hunters - ARCHAIC
lead people to AFTERWORLD, by their way of being able to leave
body.

—S.E.ASIA, S.N.AMERICA, CENTRAL ASIA.

rophet, Fool's COUSIN — ARTISTICALLY ACTIVE
(costume, masks) — Theatrical
Genius.

ve a Shaman —
~ called whether you want to or not
— Patri/lineally, Matri/lineally

— Personal Quest.

2 KINDS OF INSTRUCTION
Ecstasy ~ Dreams - VISIONS - TRANCES.

— Learned body of Knowledge, Shaman School
Know — Family Histories (Genealogy)
— Special Language

Seeks solitude, has visions, sings in sleep, Spaces out,
loses consciousness, cuts himself up
hysterical crisis

PROPENSITY TO TELL "
OR
INABILITY TO KNOW THAT
YOU'RE FUCKING UP BY TALKING
LIKE A LUNATIC.

VS. VISIONS

PROPHET

**Because we have so
little room in
our hearts for
our grief, we make
the whole world
grieve.**

- Stephen Levine

THE FOREST OF
TRUE STORIES

THE FOREST OF TRUE STORIES

In The Forest of True Stories, you have to navigate everyone's warring fucking truths forever. There's never any certainty in The Forest of True Stories. Not ever. It's nauseating, anxiety making. It's almost unbearable, the noise and the tension the true stories cause.

The Forest of True Storiess is thick with beings called "characters." You are one of these beings. Beneath trees and alongside streams, you and others like you interact as if frozen in time, waiting for the apocalypse in a public utilities commission waiting room. It is impossible to discover which character you are, until they call the number on your ticket. It's impossible to know why you're there.

Your identity is relative to your witness or accuser and therefore tactical. What is the thing beholding you?

Let's say it's an aluminum foil sculpture, twisted mindlessly, about two inches tall and four inches long from head to tail, spray painted red. It's a friend or a suicide trigger. Do you fuck it or eat it? Do you plant it and hope it will grow up into a forest that's also a time machine?

Look for the context clues. Are you its loyal subject or the one who abandons it casually, without regret? The one who gives it away, then wants it back but only as long as it's gone?

For now, in this particular configuration of forest, you want your little plaything back. The dead girl doesn't need it anymore, if she ever did.

Of course she did.

But if you should come to need him, how to find him?

After all he's only a narrative device, yet one that might help. Where would a creature of that type hide?

All you know is Blinky came from the forest and may have returned to the forest again. But now "forest" means too many things.

Still, you know that Blinky is either alive, inert, or dead. There is nothing more reliable than the difference between living and dead. There are no shades of gray. So look for something alive, inert, or dead in The Forest of True Stories, and you'll find Blinky.

You could try using the phone.

It's possible I've created an impossible truth here in The Forest of True Stories. It's possible that if he exists, he lives, dead or not or not. And he exists.

So you should look for something that exists or seems to exist.

I'm trying to connect with you, even though you're just a made-up fiction to me, like Blinky is to you. Make your own Blinky. Go to the kitchen, find a piece of garbage, and make your own Blinky. Make up your own me. Your identity is relative to the Blinky or me you conceive, so take your time.

Okay, I'm an illusion, but illusions have real effects.

Never mind though. I'm just hawking my party favors in The Forest of True Stories like every other asshole. The forest is a church. A marketplace. A magical looking glass. But I'm not standing on some riser pointing with both index fingers at my own face. Not tooting my own horn. And I'm not saying I've learned how to juggle multiple opposing truths in my mind at the same time, and I like it. Maybe Blinky's good at that, but not me. I'm no charismatic sociopath.

If I were, I would have cut down all the trees in this Forest already, and in falling they would have pounded all the other true storytellers, one by one, like nails in the ground, like cartoon railroad spikes. And then we'd all be certain and go to sleep.

And I'm not saying I've found the way, so here's the formula, get on the bus. Not at all.

All the true stories will rush at us with needful eyes and wait for us to make a choice.

Cardamom and Rosewater

Mighty Ereshkigal. Just Ereshkigal. Cool, unmovable Ereshkigal unfolded Inanna's skin and hung it from a hook near the door. On the floor, Inanna's meat pulsed beneath its layer of fat, and the organs slowed behind muscle and bone. The eyes were still.

Was her sister there?

Ereshkigal checked for signs of life.

No, there was no goddess there. No one to help her face the dread, the mountains of dream-wishes of the dead,

"Rosewater," said the dead. "Please, cardamom," they begged even in their sleep. The fucking begging dead. And no one to help.

Inanna's carcass had petaled with tears like any other.

She was mostly gone, and Ereshkigal was alone. She lay face down on her bed and tried to weep.

November 17, 1992

[Gil] left three messages for me on my roommate's machine last night.

I think she must've read that note I left in her box at school asking for the number where she was staying. I guess she had called me at work, maybe she was just outside at the pay phone. At work she called and said she was on Market Street, dying.

But the guy at the front desk didn't come and get me out of my booth and tell me she was on the phone. So I don't know. Maybe she thought I didn't want to talk to her? I don't know how to get in touch with her.

I don't know where she is. But now, I know I shouldn't try to find her, because she thinks I'm one of the enemies.

Her messages were:

First Message:

"DON'T EVEN THINK OF COMING ANYWHERE NEAR MY HOUSE, NO WAY, BABE."

Second Message:

"FUCK YOU."

Third Message:

"ARRRGHHH."

I am certainly afraid of all this.

I am certainly plagued.

She left 3 msgs on [My room mate's] phone last night. Nov 17.
I think she must've read that note I
left. At work she called & said she was
on Mkt Street dying but [The guy at the front desk] didn't come +
get me + 1. Don't even think of coming anywhere
near my house, no way babe to the please leave
a number + then 2. Fuck you 3. arrghhh.
I am certainly afraid of all this. I am
certainly plagued.

She'd been missing three days.
I was wild with worry.

Three Days

After the terror of having been skinned alive, I experienced a kind of warm thick calm, a depth of confidence. I was like the empty space between atoms. I understood transition. The moment when a carcass transforms into a habitat, the way insects find their way to its shelter and feed. I felt myself feeding there, too, all the ones I might become.

It was like being the driving force at the very center of a flax seed. There was a quietness, but also an urgency.

Somehow the seed I was made me pregnant. Remember, this is just an allegory. There's no other way to explain. I felt pregnant with my new dead self. I became a sort of home for my death, a thickening husk. And inside, a dormant seed.

I understood this without thinking: The earth, which is my body, is both grave and garden as they say. But I didn't know they meant both grave and garden at the same time.

I didn't know much, but with an intensity of certainty, I did know I had to guard my fetus with all my strength, and even without my divine powers I had all the strength of the living and dead and the force of all the space in between. I had all the strength of all the clichés and all the questions and all the undreamed perfect dreams. I had the strength to tend to my own grave where I lay curled up like a fox, dividing, dividing, dreaming. I had the strength to rest, to tend, and to wait.

After two days, I came to understand this roiling latency would never change.

It would last exactly forever. That is the defining feature of death: the end of change, the end of dying.

I would never become embodied and separate from all other being. I would never stretch out my hand and meet resistance. I would not have a conversation or smell the green breath of a cow. My tongue would never burn. I would never give birth to my dead self. The seed would stay dormant, safe. It would always remain potential.

I was free.

I was dead three days before I was rescued, and here is what I learned from it:

Freedom without form is wasted.

The Origins of Sin

On the last night that [Gil] was at my house we were tragic, as one might guess. I called her "Mother." Said I was "hers," of her womb, of her mouth. She called me "baby," "father," "brother" and "God." All characters in the giant archetypical opera coming together for a final hand-holding chorus before dropping dead, wild applause, then curtain-fall.

I tried to go down far into my psyche, so far the lights went out and there was nothing, yet still alive. Like waking up in a cave and there's nobody there, but maybe there is, so you start making sounds to check for an echo or some other clue. It's peaceful there, and it's always the same moment, so you don't feel claustrophobic or bored. Then you hear yourself saying, "I love you."

And that's how you come back. Was your lover there, too, in the emptiness with you? Were you alone? It's hard to remember now that your faces are so close and you're trying to tell one another something by the way you both hold each other so tight.

Maybe you don't know what I'm talking about which may indicate your psychic health, but still I'm sad for you if you don't. If you've never thought you might be in the cave and she's with you in there, too. Sometimes you just slip into glossolalia and so does she, and it's like you just keep switching the frequencies, dialing up or dialing down the sound patterns, hoping for a fit between your two secret languages. And sometimes it fits and you cry.

If it's possible for people to really understand each other, then any type of magic might be real. Jesus and fairies and outer space worlds might be. Radical transformation might be possible. The end of capitalism and charismatic leaders with final solutions and blood revolutions. Plus, other even more fantastical things.

I mean to say there might be a better world, it might be real. A secret world unlocked and revealed in glimpses, in sound bytes along an invisible cable, a chord between two people when they're fucking or meditating or whatever. Undermining language somehow.

I mean there is a sort of language, but it is spoken between the cells and organs and all the other forsaken entities and ecosystems that make up what passes for a unified form, a sack of a body with a green-winged soul stuffed inside a tiny circus cage and a mind like a mustachioed ringmaster tapping his toe at the top.

When we were laying in my bed for the last time before [Gil] disappeared, she asked me for something.

She said she wanted me to give her something. It was, she knew, the most tempting gift she could offer: a request for my help. I didn't know that yet, but she did. She knew about girls like me. So I did it exactly the way she asked me to. It hurt me, and I did it. I took the scalpel and cut straight into her wrist. I cut the symbol of "Sin" there. It looked like a moon on its back. Afraid and charged, I got high cutting her. Maybe she'd bleed to death while she slept. I tried to cut deep enough to make the scar but not to hit a vein. I didn't know what specific stamp of sin she was asking me to brand her with. I didn't ask.

That is who I had become. I licked her wound and went to sleep with her arm wrapped around me and her chest pressed into my back.

I licked her wound before she could stop me, I sucked it, and then went to sleep.

Do you think she tried to stop me? Do you?

I found something strange the next morning. On a page in my journal she had written, "Run For Your Life."

Do you think she meant to protect me?

THE FOREST OF GOOD BAD INTENTIONS

In The Forest of Good Bad Intentions, close counts like horseshoes. Phone booths red with scratched up glass grow up from the forest floor, taller than a man. Other colors, too, all shapes and sizes, some with benches, some without. Inside them phones are ringing, phones are ringing. It's a warning. Is it? A message, a sign. Which one? Look for clues, a bloody handprint on the receiver, a single baby shoe outside the door. Pull the door, the doors, go in. Say, "Hello?"

The forest is thick and loud; it's humid. Moist desperate air. Everything living is still, except for the phones who are crying, they will not be soothed. It's deafening, headachy buzz. This forest of perversions where a girl goes searching for the right phone the wrong way, feeling her way from caller to caller, her intuition shot through with sound.

She doesn't even know what she's looking for. Something else, a decoder ring, something. Different, better. True. Some undeniable encounter. The audio physical fact that will change everything. The one to Narnia or the mothership. The time machine, the father's love, the pill that melts slowly on the tongue.

The phones are screaming in bells, the phone booths shiver like boughs. Bird shit drips in something like patterns.

In this forest, yes, the girl confronts her choices, but they don't feel like choices. All the phone booths look the same, picking one seems arbitrary, aesthetic, the green one the blue one the one with broken glass like tears or teeth on its floor. Pick the prettiest one. Pick the ugliest one. Try, try harder. There is some urgency. It is a test. A game.

She could leave at any time.

One caller says: We all want to kill. Find the caller who wants to be killed. The girl drops the phone, it dangles and spins. Is it true? Do I want to feel life slowly ebb in my hand, is that love, could I give someone that?

She tongues the holes in the receiver for clues, feels her taste buds drag into the little holes, tastes salt and copper.

One caller says: there is no way to be good in a world of concepts and meat. Find the caller who'll never be good and thank the caller for being forthcoming.

One caller says: I want you to kill me. Come find me. Carve the symbol of sin into my wrist, suck the blood. Watch yourself do it, watch yourself cut a perfect arc and dip your mouth into the pool and drink until you're sleepy.

She taps the receiver against her forehead, taps it, trying to remember something, then harder, thinks this is stupid, then drops it, pushes out the booth. Which way?

One caller says: Find the broken-wing bird chirping weakly from somewhere it can't describe. Whisper sweetly into its ear hole hidden by miniscule feathers. Whisper the thing that will make it drift into sleep. Its wing will heal while it sleeps, and it will fly in the morning and ride on your shoulder forever, picking dandruff from your hair.

Close. And close counts.

One caller says: Here, read my journal. I want you to know everything about me, I want you to trust me. I'm here. On the page. I want you to see me. Don't look at me. Read my journal. No secrets, see? See everything. Agree. Agree you see me.

She opens the torn-up phone book expecting to find love there, a number to call. Someone on the other end who'll both listen and respond. The pages are crinkled as if they've fallen into a pool and dried. She dials a number, hears a phone ring nearby.

The one who answers says: There's a book for everything. Find the caller with the largest most secret sacred library and convince the caller to give you a key. Stay there in the library until you know everything in the books, don't come out before you're done or no one will see you anymore. Make sure you finish. You will have to learn many languages first, old ones and made-up ones, ones made of wrinkles, invisible ones. You will have to learn them all. When you finish reading the last book in the library, find the caller who will ask you a question, the one you could not have answered before, then answer the question. Elaborate. Let your elaboration become a book. Return to the library and place the book on its shelf.

Phones spinning on their stretchy metal cords, undone, unrung, answered, dying, yearning.

One caller says: Young lady, this is your mother. March yourself home right now. Find the caller who knows where home is. Find one you can believe. Don't trust strangers.

The girl looks for a stranger, but she is alone in the forest of good bad intentions. Except for the ringing. The disembodied voices.

Her body reacts, pushing wetness from pores and ducts. What's inside her skin seeps outside, rests on her skin, coating her in sticky patches. Her face is wet, her feet are wet, her panties, her palms, her hair.

One caller says: Find the red flashing button and push it. No one will remember a thing. Utopia, clean green slate. Do it. Please do it. Please do it. I'm begging.

So close.

One caller says: Lay thee down now and rest. May thy slumber be blessed. Lay thee down now and rest, may thy slumber be blessed.

She gives up. Falls down. Stays, tries to nap. Her heart pounds and drowns out the phones. She says to herself, "The dwarves. The dwarves will find me and take me to their cabin and I will clean it for them and make curtains." She waits for the dwarves to get out of the mines. Covers her ears with both hands.

The phone booths seem to multiply: thick ones, thin ones, ones from Europe and Japan. Long swathes of rectangular shade merging on the ground, and cigarette butts, bits of newspaper stick to the syrup on their floors. Smell of piss, old wallets, of aspirin, gardenias.

The next caller says: Find the right agent. You've got star potential, you're a natural. You know it, I know it, and every asshole on every phone in this forest knows it. You're the one. The ONE. Find the caller who'll represent you, get you a good deal.

One caller says: Vanity of vanities, all is vanity. What profit hath man for all his labours under the sun?

One caller says: Wanna come over and party? We've got everything, piles of it. Everyone's asking for you.

She looks for the party. She can't hear the music. She's lost, deep in the Forest of Good Bad Intentions. It stretches around her for thousands of miles. She gives up again. Tries. Gives up. Picks a vintage Bell booth, toothy chrome.

That caller says: Everyone you've talked with so far is a liar. They want you to fuck them, they'll say anything. And you want to fuck them so you'll just keep answering phones. You're a liar like them. That's you on the phone. They're all you.

One caller says: Find the blackest bruise on your throat. Press on it. Hit it with a small silver hammer. It hurts to get your attention. Don't be distracted. Don't hear the ringing. Don't you dare drop this phone.

So she stands there listening to the dead air, listening hard, waiting. There's nothing else to do for now but listen, press the bruise and wait like a bride for her own attention to come to her like a ranger on horseback. She uses the hammer. It hurts and she feels it. She waits, not daring to drop this phone.

Dead air.

Closer still.

In the Forest of Good Bad Intentions, the girl will misplace and replace her makeshift faith, pain to pain, plan to plan, phone to phone, trying and giving up and trying again. The girl will try anything. On one of the phones, a direct line to God.

Not Any Enemy

When the phone finally rang, I tripped over cords, running to the front room to get it. I'd been waiting and waiting for the phone to ring.

"Hello? [Gil]?"

Her voice, hovering as a sheet-ghost said, "I've warned the nurses about you."

[Gil] hadn't called for days, not since she'd tried to jump off the first roof. Since then she'd been spotted hobbling up Mission and on a bus headed toward the Golden Gate Bridge.

I told [Gil] I didn't have any spies, wouldn't go looking for her: "I'm your girlfriend not some enemy." But [Gil] was pursued no matter what. She always got away just in time. That was half her charm.

November 15, 1992

Dear Nina (remember this for later),

    Tonight you were watching Slacker when [Gil] called and told you she was in the Psyche Ward at General. She explained what happened over the last few days while she was missing.

    She told you that she saw you or a person resembling you, the way you put your hair up, across the street at 23rd and Guerrero, up in the window of the flat across the street, and that there was a man who came to the room you were in and then a flurry of packing. Then 2 girls packed some video equipment that [Gil] thought was being used to tape her.

    She said this is why she left those strange messages on the answering machine, because she thought you were part of the group who'd been following her. She asked, "Are you sure?" The girl in the apartment had your hair. She was certain the girl was you.

    You tried to sound reassuring. You listened and tried not to sound accusatory.

    She said that she had been staying with her ex-girlfriend, Malena. Malena's roommate was also one of her drug dealer's customers. She said this roommate listened in on [Gil]'s phone calls, and when she was talking about you (she wouldn't say what it was) to some friend, the roommate was listening on the other line and said, "Oh, that's perfect," as if to imply it was obvious to everyone that you were somehow involved in the conspiracy against her. So then she believed the whole relationship had been a setup from the beginning.

    And she said that, as she lay there hearing voices saying, "Kill her, kill her," her dealer and his friend came up the stairwell but did not come into the room she was in. They talked loudly about how they should break her other leg. Then they left the house.

    She slept holding her knife, just in case.

    When Malena came home and asked what was happening and [Gil] tried to explain, Malena told [Gil] she had to get out of the house. So [Gil] tried to make her way (on one broken leg) down toward Alternative University so she could sleep there. (She has a key.)

While she was walking down Valencia, a black car driven by her drug dealer pulled up alongside her, hit her in the other leg, then left.

She did not tell you whether or not they said anything to her as they hit her. She then crawled all the way to the college and climbed the stairs to our professor's office, which was unlocked, and went in there to sleep.

The next morning she began to yell at the people from the Weekend College seated below the window because she heard them telling her to jump. Then she went out onto the balcony because one challenged her, saying something like, "Yeah, so what are you gonna do about it?"

She stood up there on the landing and heard everyone yelling for her to jump, which she thought was strange since she hadn't even considered it until the people started telling her to.

Then the German girl across the street asked her to come down and said she would bring some coffee, and so [Gil] went down. Three different students had called the police who questioned her and then declared her 5150. So now she'd be held for 72 hours there at General until they could figure out what to do with her.

She is convinced that her dealer is trying to drive her to suicide because he is a bigtime dealer and she has proven she isn't loyal to him, which makes her dangerous. He just got out of jail after doing seven years for trafficking, and she has already had lots of encounters with the police in the past few weeks, so it makes sense that he would want to threaten or kill her, in case she's been telling the cops about him, because if he goes back to jail, it's his third strike.

She doesn't know what to do about this, because it'll just start up again when she gets out of the hospital.

She said that somebody (her brother?) is sending her a gun. Which, if it happens, terrifies you.

She asked you to quit your job at the peepshow, and you said no.

She said, "Then I can't dance with you."

You said, "I know."

Later in the conversation she said that you two could no longer have sex, and you said you knew that, too.

She asked you how you knew that, and you said, "Well, you just asked me to quit my job and I said no, and you don't want to be with someone who does the work I do."

She said no, it wasn't that. It was because she had tested positive for HIV. She repeated the word "positive" three times.

"Positive. Positive. Positive."

When you asked how long she had known, she said, "For a little while." She said that's why she kept asking you to get tested. She said this many times.

She started crying, and then she apologized, and you said it was okay, and you consoled her. You told her you loved her. She was afraid you wouldn't want to talk to her anymore, and you said you would never stop talking to her, and you would do everything you could to help her, always. You don't know why you said this.

You said you'd get tested then go visit her. She would need to tell you where she was staying.

Now you want to take something that will make you sleep for days. You don't have anything. You are afraid she will shoot everyone if she gets a gun and they let her out on the street. You believe this. You don't know who to talk to.

Tomorrow you will get tested.

You have done some fucking stupid things.

You wonder if she making this up?

You wonder if you will die soon.

You think it might be possible that her dealer drove up and hit her leg.

Love, You

The Flies

Flies, as you know, come and go between the underworld and living Earth. They keep the dead company until the corpses become seeds.

My companion Ninshubur rescued me, as planned. She sent two crafty flies down to help. They found my sister moaning and pulling at her hair in anguish, and they moaned along with her. She felt so grateful for their empathy, she offered them whatever they wanted. So they took me.

I had to find someone to replace me, and Ninshubur offered herself, of course, as she would. She is very loving, but doesn't always think much of herself. I said no, I loved her too much.

But, Gilgamesh, I returned to the world of the living frazzled and changed. My death made me see the world so differently, I had become undefined, and it was horribly uncomfortable. By now I was used to pain, but I still had no acceptance of it. Even with all my strength, I could not pull myself together. I wandered through the City looking for someone to replace me in the underworld.

In the marketplace, I saw the common dread of ending, of losing, the fear of making mistakes. I saw bodies aging, plants withering, dogs with silver muzzles and cloudy eyes. I heard coughing and watched ants drowning in spilled juice. I saw danger everywhere, and I was anxious, not for myself, but for the ones who would mourn the passing of time, of change, as they waited, pregnant and peaceful, forever.

It would be a beautiful feeling, and I saw people leaning toward it in various haphazard ways. The opium smokers, the ascetics and the vengeful soldiers, the handless thieves and the most brutal kings leaned into sweet and false dormancy. In their violence and violent bliss they found temporary peace in imaginary homes until they no longer had the ability to choose. They had lost themselves to their thirst, but the water they drank dried their mouths. They became so parched, they drank more and more, until they were nothing but thirst itself.

And still they kept their form, and still they were situated in time. Still they could affect one another and change. They'd know true dissolution soon enough.

I envied the brutes and the addicts for their inventiveness.

The heaviness of this new death wisdom upset me. I felt lost even with all my power restored. I searched for someone to take my place in the underworld, because that was the deal. But no matter who I came across, I saw the fullness of their lives, the preciousness of their time in a body, and I could not find one that deserved to die more than any other. I resented the living for making me weak. The feeling of skinlessness returned, and I was repulsed by the foolish brightness of life.

I did not recognize myself. I needed to be comforted. I went in search of my Dumuzi.

You know what happened then. The story of my great betrayal of Dumuzi is well-known. It's why you don't want to marry me. You know I sent my most beloved shepherd to his death.

I saw him near our home, sitting under the apple tree, so beautiful and brown, his hands so fine, his hair so curly. He wore his best clothes and his feet were clean and oiled. There were girls surrounding him laughing at his stories. He sipped from a wineskin as if on a festival day. He seemed truly joyous. He was not mourning my death. In that moment I died all over again.

I could not stop myself. It was like my heart was being squeezed until it was empty, limp, and used. I would do anything to rid myself of the pain. From that seat of torture I sent my lover to die.

What I did not know until many years later was this: My urgency to punish Dumuzi was the same force that caused him to so desperately distract himself with light pleasures. And it is the same force that makes great leaders into brutal tyrants. Everyone wants the discomfort to go.

But listen closely, Gilgamesh.

Anna Joy Springer

Dying gave me only partial knowledge of death. When they took my husband's body away, I learned the greater truth of it.

The process of dying is terrifying and often painful, but it ends. The dead are not in pain, they're safe. The dead know no war and no complicated love. There is no time and no form. They dissolve into vast potential.

The ones who know the great sorrow of death are the ones who remain alive to mourn. Grief is all the living know of death. And grief, let me tell you, is unbearable. It never fully passes. When someone we love dies, the one we had become in relation to them also dies, but we're forced to stay alive with this dead part inside. We fear, in finally dying, we will be forced grieve our own loss plus the loss of all we love for all eternity.

It's grief we fear most, not death.

November 18, 1992

Dear me, dear me, dear me:

Poor [Gil] calls and says you are sweet, and is alone again where she will always be and now you feel sorry for her.

She has the disease and your sorrow is separate from its pertinence to you. It is so appropriate to her life's story, and soon she will have to mourn her mortality and perhaps think of her future and her desires and be active.

There is a deadline now for her, and perhaps for you too. Still it seems so far away from possible, but you know it is not and you can't even be afraid, it sounds so distant and fake, but you really are and lordgod this is very real, much more than the way you've been telling people, like repeating a television episode or another exaggerated lie, like the hunchback lie you used to tell your friends when you were a kid.

Dumuzi Returns

Yes, Dumuzi returns each spring, but he doesn't come to me. He has never forgiven me for what I did.

I have distributed all of my powers but one. The power I want is something none of the gods understand. They have everything one could want, but they suffer, too.

Have you come up with the answer to my question, Gilgamesh? If you answer correctly, I will give you my last, most sought-after power.

Shall I offer you another clue?

She who will never die cannot experience it, and she who is all powerful cannot, either. She who avoids going into the forest alone cannot. She who has no body cannot. She who believes she is separate from all being cannot, but neither can she who denies her separateness.

She who successfully clings to pleasure and flees from pain and she who battles change and forces certainty won't experience it. She who has deafened herself against the cries of wounded animals, plants and minerals cannot, nor can she who ignores her own cries. She who is too full of pride to let her self disintegrate into love, and she who will not allow her self die a little with every breath, will likely not experience this state I desire so deeply.

I don't know if it lasts or comes in flashes. I would do anything to feel it for just one moment. But I cannot. To experience this state of union with the divine, you have to know that you will finally and irrevocably die, and that everything you love and hate will someday disappear.

Let me tempt you, King, with my own immortality.

December 5, 1992

[Gil]'s poetry nemesis professor called her shrink and asked if she were truly HIV+. Her shrink didn't answer but then called [Gil] and told her that the professor had called.

She was upset that I hadn't come to visit her yet.

Last night at work Star and I kissed, then fucked. Now I have bite welts on my neck. Star uses heroin and she has sex with a lot of people. It wasn't safe sex, that is dumb, more than dumb.

God, when will I get a clue?

I remember being shocked learning that when they were testing the atomic bomb, the guy doing it told the newspaper that there was a three-in-a-million chance the explosion would set the nitrogen in the atmosphere on fire, and it would fry the whole planet, but that, to him, seemed a reasonable chance to take.

December 16, 1992

[Gil]'s serious about ending her life, though I don't know how. She wanted to talk about it. She's probably writing a lot. She's got a vendetta. She's betrayed by the group, the people at school, me, everyone.

That's what she thinks, ever since her professor called her shrink to find out if it's true or not that she's positive. I don't even know the name of her shrink.

Yes, we fucked two times and it was good. She made sure we used protection. It was sad.

I remember very little about the visit. I lied to her the whole time. Nothing was there but my want, my fucking bottomless want.

I never knew her, never thought to want to know her.

Perhaps I'm going to become very depressed very soon.

Maybe [Gil] will be dead in a little while, and when she's gone I won't be able to talk to her ghost because she thinks I'm seeing someone else, and so she won't come.

Anna Joy Springer

THE NOT FAKE PARALLEL FOREST

With such a pair as we were, was love possible?

[leaves flutter]

Was our forest ever compassionate?

[an animal howls]

Did our forest reaffirm the belief that real communication is impossible?

[footsteps]

Did our made-up composite forest help some creatures touch, in some sort of forest somewhere, and not fake and not because it's recorded?

[a sharpness that corkscrews through an organ without mass]

[yes, that]

January 16, 2007

I see that I went to visit [Gil] one last time on April 20, 1993, to bring her some food. She'd called and asked me to come. Blinky was there in her bed, I remember that clearly now.

She said, "You know you're pathetic when Nina brings you groceries."

It was the day after the FBI killed seventy-five people, including twenty-one children in the Branch Dividian raid in Waco, Texas. The FBI said they didn't shoot fire or inflammatory grenades into the building, but later it came out that they had. That's what they do, fuck people up and lie about it. That's their job. Again, when you've got all the guns why not just say it? I'm still confused about that.

[Gil] had been glued to the television for 50 days, watching the coverage, trying to decide whether or not to buy a bus ticket and go there herself.

She knew what was going on in that compound. She knew what Koresh would be saying and how scared everyone would be. For them, this was the apocalypse.

And she knew what was going on outside the building, too. Most we could see on TV, but [Gil] was prophetic: She said the FBI would burn the whole thing down to get rid of the evidence of the shootings. And they did burn it down.

Lots of little cult kids died. Adults were afraid that if they ran out of the building they'd be shot. And children were afraid that if they ran out their mothers would be arrested and they'd be taken and put with strangers who hated God. Because that's what had happened to the other kids who'd left. Most of the kids had decided to stay in the building throughout the standoff. They'd been told they could leave at any time. They didn't want to leave their parents. They stayed of their own free will.

The day before -- day 51 of the standoff -- [Gil] was going to get on the bus. That was the day the whole thing blew up, so there was nowhere go to, except for the ruins.

[Gil]'s apartment room was dark, even though it was afternoon. I watched the post-massacre footage with her, then I left. I didn't know what to do for her. And she'd told me to run for my life.

She didn't kill herself for two more years.

The Answer's Not Really An Answer At All

Gilgamesh answered Inanna's question confidently, and his answer was perfect. Although he didn't believe her, he had heard what she was getting at.

So, as Inanna had promised, she drew him a map to the herb of everlasting life. It was the last plant of its kind, and by eating it Gilgamesh would never die. He would become a god. It was growing just outside the first gate of the underworld. He left the Temple to find Enkidu and prepare for their adventure to go find the plant. He would share the herb with his friend and they would be gods together.

Inanna readied herself for her own journey. She gave her place in the sky to a beautiful spinning planet that rose and set with the sun, as she had. She surrendered all Temple affairs to those Priestesses who enjoyed political power. She invited any woman who would like it to join her on her journey.

So, Inanna, her companion Ninshubur, and the twelve whores walked for weeks over rough and varied terrain. Their clothes were torn and their skin was blistered when they arrived at a small river village near an enormous broadleaf forest.

Inanna asked the villagers for permission to make a home in the forest.

"Why would you do such a thing?" the people asked.

Inanna answered, "We are trying to learn how to be both free and alive at the same time."

The villagers gave the women permission to live in the forest and offered to bring them food.

At the edge of the forest, Inanna stood still and felt her self small and breathing. The women around her became quiet.

They watched her. She stood still for a long time, facing the forest.

Then Inanna removed her crown and set it on a flat stone at the head of the trail into the forest. She removed her short strand of lapis beads and set it down. She removed her double strand of carnelian beads and set it down. She removed her breastplate and set it down. Inanna removed her gold owl ring and set it down, too. She set down on the stone her measuring rod and line. She paused.

She asked her friends to help her remove her royal robe. Some of them began to cry. The robe fell to the ground like a husk. Inanna wrapped herself in a long piece of smooth beige cloth.

Then she walked into the impossible forest. A strange bird made a strange scream.

Strategy Games Go On Forever

When [Gil] got pneumonia from the HIV, she did a giant speedball and died. Her girlfriend had just left her and she told the girlfriend, "I'm going to kill myself if you leave." But she had always said that. She'd said it to me.

Love was antithetical, so hatred was disguised as love.

I hadn't believed her. I didn't believe myself, either. What I'd felt was love. I'd thought it was love.

By the time she succeeded in killing herself, I hadn't seen her in over a year – still pissed that she'd known she was positive the whole time we were together and never told me. I knew she was sick and might die. I believed I was beyond caring. She was already as good as dead. I was tough and realistic. I'd learned the truth of what I was. And she had tried to murder me. Me.

How had I come to care whether I lived or not? When had I changed, behind my own back? How had I crossed over into the world of people who want to win, away from the ones like [Gil], who just can't take it one more god damned second? And why did it happen to me, not to her?

I get what makes us all the same. But what eerie combination of chemicals and history make us so different from one another?

I am not better than she was. I didn't deserve to escape more than she did.

The Epic Of The Other

Enkidu grew sicker and died.

Gilgamesh ached. He carved the final version of *The Epic of Enkidu* into a flat lapis stone, blue dust settling on the tops of his feet.

If you locate the hidden copper box in a nook buried in the wall of Uruk, open the box and pull out the stone. You can read *The Epic of Enkidu* in its entirety:

Enkidu came from far away.
He was [brave].
He was [beautiful].
He was [magnificent].
He [had a brilliant mind].
He [taught me so much].

He was my friend.
He [changed me].
I loved him.
I love him still.

Gilgamesh gave the herb to a snake instead of taking it himself. He died over forty years later.

Anna Joy Springer

Why Go On

To be love's body?
The truth, [admit it], given limbs.

Feel them.

Throb. Dull. Awful. Soar.
To watch with love, alongside,
through it, of it. It, alive.

Or else the body's less than a rock,
merely [dumb starving] idea.

To offer a body to a word?
"Eat this," and hand the self away
to the shared, howling extension.

Then the [bitter/sweet] return:
little crab apple with insect wings.

Just this? [Yes this.]
This shared and unrequited love.

January 30, 2007

I ended our friendship over the telephone. It was the middle of the day, and I was sitting in my new girlfriend's apartment at her desk.

I cut [Gil] off, saying, "I don't think I can be friends with someone who tried to kill me."

I broke my promise.

I didn't want to die.

I was supposed to be a strong feminist who took care of herself.

I was supposed to respect myself.

I wasn't supposed to be friends with people who hurt me.

I ended our friendship over the phone.

[Gil] died in battle, let's say.

There are some warriors I can't help but defend. Having sprung from her father's head, adult, untouchable, and in full armor.

Where Is Blinky?

When she killed her dying self, when she made that choice of choices, Blinky wrote and told me that he was sick, too.

Totally betrayed by this information, not having the disease myself, still I went to visit him, bring him food. But he had already descended into the shadowy world with the pills and feathery comforter pulled all around.

As he got sicker, he stopped blinking and then even stopped curling up his nose.

I didn't want him to be there alone in the horrifying apartment and sick so far from home. So I took him with me. I kept him.

When he died, I planted him deep in the ground so he would grow tall and strong.

You can't water things with your tears.

That's a lie.

No Escape Hatch In the Forest

She came straight at me, decomposing in too many ways to resist, scribbling these angelic forms into my notebook. Eyeing me.

And the big unspoken law of battle: That the stretch of kindness is equal to the pressure of aggression. And meets it neck and neck. We wander through this dream, watching for clues, can't shake the suspicion that it is a murder mystery we're all starring in, can't shake the fascination of driving by slowly, craning our necks. Or even stop and gawk, or even do it tenderly. And hear something calling to us.

Who is it we hear?

Are you with me or are you against me?

[Gil] held herself differently at different times, a great actor in her different roles. Who we think we are, we become seen to be. Or vice-versa. In one scenario her father was a monster, then a caricature, or a ghostly figment. Marching, searching for some great and solid thing to be.

And I say, "Knock knock."

"Who's there?"

"Unrequited love."

I love it but it won't ask me, "Unrequited love, who?"

And it won't answer, either.

Sometimes, in my dreams, I feel it in my heart – that I would give everything to get her back. Not back, but alive, and different this time.

Some kind of ancient, antiquated earplug falls out. It's a whole new kind of story, not a tragedy, not a comedy where the heroine overcomes many hardships and sucks on her candy ring in front of crowds and crowds of awestruck peasants while the wedding bells go crazy. Something different this time, more classy this time. Not too freaked out, and with better drugs. But I'm asleep, it's when I dream.

God damn it, a whore can be anything. A father can be anything. A forest, a teacher. Anything. I relax, look into the word, and when I try to find what the word is pointing to, I never can find it. It's moving too fast or I'm moving too fast. Still haunted, though, I long. Keep searching, keep stalking, but I never can find the damn thing.

What was it I was looking for, again?

This unrequited love, but not so grim. Not meant to be, it never dies, this yearning for the truest, most unguarded.

I feel tender toward something as close as my own heart, but it recedes.

Underfoot twigs break quietly. Danger all around us, ego danger, red, I tell myself: Keep stalking.

201

I know you can still hear me.

About The Author

Anna Joy Springer is a prose writer and visual artist who makes grotesques – creating hybrid texts that combine sacred and profane elements to evoke intensely embodied conceptual-emotional experiences in readers. Formerly a singer in the Bay Area bands, Blatz, The Gr'ups, and Cypher in the Snow, Anna Joy has toured the United States and Europe being a wild feminist punk performer, and also toured with the all-women spoken word extravaganza, Sister Spit. She is author of the illustrated novella, *The Birdwisher* (Birds of Lace). She received her MFA in Literary Arts from Brown University, and is now Associate Professor of Literature at University of California at San Diego, where she truly loves teaching courses in Experimental Writing, Graphic Texts, and Postmodern Feminist Literatures.

1831020R00107

Made in the USA
San Bernardino, CA
06 February 2013